"Professor Peter Marina Ph.D. and Police Lt. Pedro Marina (Ret.) capture the true essence of servant leadership and routinely exemplify a compassionate approach to every aspect of law enforcement. Their masterful work, *Emergency Dispatch and Human Rights: Before the Sirens,* highlights a critical yet historically understudied point of intervention—the moment when emergency dispatchers first engage with individuals in crisis.

By bringing the importance of accurate, compassionate, and human rights-centered emergency dispatch to the forefront, the authors illuminate a vital component of public safety that has too often been overlooked. This book is an essential read for law enforcement professionals, emergency dispatchers, first responders, policymakers, and anyone dedicated to applying human rights principles to real-world scenarios. With provided insights and commitment a new heightened standard for ethical policing will emerge ensuring that crisis response is as effective, humane, compassionate, and safe as possible from the all important initial contact to ultimate remedy."

Chief Joel E. Gordon *(Ret.)*
BLUE Magazine Editor-in-Chief

Emergency Dispatch and Human Rights

Through real calls, field narratives, and thinkers from Du Bois and Weber to Simmel and Foucault, this book reframes the dispatcher's role from a clerical function to a moral one.

Dispatchers make split-second decisions that impact the fate of everyone a call involves, yet they remain the most consequential and least examined actors in policing. Sociologist Peter J. Marina draws on urban ethnography, social theory, and the 30 years of street-level law enforcement experience of retired New Orleans Police Department (NOPD) Lieutenant Pedro Marina to argue that human rights protection begins not when officers arrive, but the moment someone answers the phone. The blasé attitude, warrior and guardian orientations, the sociological imagination, dual-subject asymmetry, and tri-subject asymmetry all converge at the dispatch console, where a single framing decision determines how the caller is heard, how the officer understands the situation, and how the silent subject who never speaks is ultimately treated. A 5-year-old named Tia Hernlen, a woman whispering from a locked bathroom, a jogger stopped for existing while Black, and the Trayvon Martin case all ask the same question. Will the dispatcher see all three: the caller who speaks, the person who never does, and the officer heading toward a scene?

The book will be of interest to emergency service dispatchers, non-dispatch supervisors/managers, and students in criminal justice or emergency service programs, as well as those involved in policymaking, training, and implementation within policing organizations.

Peter Marina is a New Orleans native, sociologist, and criminologist, and Associate Professor of Sociology and Criminology. Trained at the New School for Social Research, Marina's scholarship focuses on urban ethnography, transgression, and social inequalities, with particular attention to human rights, policing, and communities living on society's margins. He is the author of *Human Rights Policing*, *Down and Out* *in New Orleans* and several other books and articles. Marina's thinking examines power, resistance, and social control across diverse social worlds, from Pentecostal tongue-speaking churches and Caribbean ritual life to street performers and urban occultists.

Pedro Marina is a retired lieutenant with the New Orleans Police Department who served for more than 30 years in patrol, narcotics, robbery investigations, vice operations, and SWAT. A sociology graduate of the University of New Orleans, he held supervisory and command positions throughout New Orleans, including in the French Quarter, and received numerous commendations for exemplary service during his career. Lieutenant Marina lives in New Orleans, Louisiana, with his dog, Meggie.

Routledge Series on Practical and Evidence-Based Policing

Books in the Routledge Series on Practical and Evidence-Based Policing disseminate knowledge and provide practical tools for law enforcement leaders and personnel to protect and serve the public and reduce crime. With an aim to bridge the "translation gap" between frontline policing and academic research, books in this series apply sound scientific methods as well as practical experience to make everyday police work safer and smarter. These books are an invaluable resource for police practitioners, academic researchers, public policymakers, and students in law enforcement and criminology programs to guide best practices in all aspects of policing.

Understanding Police Operational Performance
James E. McCabe, Paul E. O'Connell, Demosthenes Long, and Carol Rasor-Cordero

Cutting Crime Using the Rule of the Few
Shannon Linning, Daniel W. Gerard and John E. Eck

Future Policing
Technology and Transformation
Laura Huey, Lorna Ferguson and Ian T. Adams

The Art of Career Advancement for Law Enforcement and Public Safety Leaders
Mastering the Seven Pillars of Professional Readiness
Jonni Redick and Erik Fritsvold

Emergency Dispatch and Human Rights
Before the Sirens
Peter Marina and Pedro Marina

Emergency Dispatch and Human Rights

Before the Sirens

Peter Marina and Pedro Marina

Routledge
Taylor & Francis Group
NEW YORK AND LONDON

Designed cover image: Getty Images

First published 2027
by Routledge
605 Third Avenue, New York, NY 10158

and by Routledge
4 Park Square, Milton Park, Abingdon, Oxon, OX14 4RN

Routledge is an imprint of the Taylor & Francis Group, an informa business

For Product Safety Concerns and Information please contact our EU representative GPSR@taylorandfrancis.com. Taylor & Francis Verlag GmbH, Kaufingerstraße 24, 80331 München, Germany.

ISBN: 978-1-032-95239-0 (hbk)
ISBN: 978-1-032-95142-3 (pbk)
ISBN: 978-1-003-58386-8 (ebk)

DOI: 10.4324/9781003583868

Typeset in Sabon
by Apex CoVantage, LLC

For the dispatchers, responders, and all whose humanity calls them to witness and to act, honoring the ordinary deeds that make human rights real.

For the humans who understand that human rights, despite their name, belong to all of God's creatures.

For the animals who will forever be denied the rights born to them, yet whose lives remind us of the work still to be done.

Contents

Contributors

Allen Hill began his law enforcement career with the Texas Highway Patrol as a state trooper before moving into university policing. He served as Police Chief at the University of Houston-Clear Lake and later at the University of Wisconsin-La Crosse, spending more than three decades moving through the institutional architecture of American law enforcement. He holds a bachelor's degree in Criminal Justice from Midwestern State University in Texas.

Mike Valencia (Ret.) served the La Crosse County Sheriff's Office for 28 years, retiring as a lieutenant in investigations. Over the course of his career he worked as a jail officer, patrol officer, training officer, and supervisor of patrol and investigations. He was a member and team leader of his department's SWAT team and is a certified trainer by the Wisconsin Department of Justice.

Preface

Why We Wrote This Book and How

This book began on a Philadelphia sidewalk, a few feet past a man saying he was dying.

It continued on a Brooklyn street where a car hit a girl and the city kept moving. It deepened across 30 years of law enforcement in New Orleans, through homicide scenes and narcotics chases and Sunday morning backlogs and a dispatcher who learned a young officer's name years before she needed it to save his life. It developed further in human rights training in Wisconsin, where law enforcement officers started skeptical but left with something unexpected to take home. It arrived, finally, at the dispatch center, where one person answers the phone while someone else's world comes apart. The dispatcher decides how much that life will matter.

We are a sociologist and a retired law enforcement lieutenant. We are also a father and a son. As a kid, I spent years sitting across from my father while he was working detail as a police officer at the McDonald's on Canal Street in New Orleans, doing something we never named but never stopped doing. We would watch the customers and quietly try to figure them all out. We would analyze their clothes, their posture, the way they carried themselves, the look behind their eyes. My father told me every person has a story, our job is to figure out that story. Where did they come from? What brought them to this city, this street, this establishment on this afternoon? What did their lives ask of them to get here? What decisions brought them to this place at this moment? My father didn't specifically call it sociology to me at the time. We just did it together, naturally, organically, like breathing. But it was on Canal Street, the street where I was born, inside that loud, rough and tough McDonald's, where my father imparted the sociological imagination upon me, where he handed me the lens I would spend the rest of my life looking through. We played this game throughout our entire lives together, including our travels to Cuba, Mexico, Peru, Spain, Portugal, Argentina, Uruguay, and Ireland, among other places. We still play it. I think we were just born sociologists.

We wrote our first book together, *Human Rights Policing: Reimagining Law Enforcement in the 21st Century*, out of a shared conviction that the principles governing how institutions treat people in their worst moments matter. People make decisions under pressure and within institutions that rarely reward acts of love, kindness, compassion, and empathy. This book extends that conviction to emergency communication, to the dispatchers who sit at the hinge between a person in crisis and everything that follows, and whose authority over human rights outcomes impacts everyone involved in an emergency call.

We wrote it because that authority remains underexamined. Scholarship on policing and human rights focuses overwhelmingly on what happens in the field, on the officer at the door, the use of force, the arrest, the encounter. The dispatcher who frames the call before anyone arrives, who shapes what officers believe they were walking into, who decides whether a caller's fear is treated as real or filed as routine, appears in that literature as background, as infrastructure, as the voice on the radio. This book argues that the dispatcher is the first and most consequential point of contact in someone's worst moment, and that human rights protection begins at the dispatch before any unit rolls.

We also wrote it because dispatchers deserve better than they receive from the institutions that depend on them and the people they serve. They absorb catastrophe through a headset, hour after hour, year after year, without the physical movement that gives officers a momentary sense of intervention, without the closure that comes from following a situation through to its resolution, and without the structured support that the emotional toll of the work demands. We take our hats off to the dispatcher and hope to serve the profession. The dispatcher – the one who protects the human rights of the caller, the subject of the call, and the responders – deserves respect.

A Note on Method

This book draws on multiple ways of knowing, and readers deserve an account of how they work together. The sociological analyses that run through these chapters draw on Peter Marina's decades of ethnographic and academic research, Pedro Marina's 30 years of practitioner experience in law enforcement, and a shared commitment to understanding what institutions do to people in their most vulnerable moments.

The personal narratives are a different kind of evidence. Both authors write from their personal experiences. The Philadelphia sidewalk, the Bergen Street incident, the girl on Atlantic Avenue, and Pedro Marina's 30 years on the streets of New Orleans serve as autoethnographic accounts, a recognized methodological tradition in sociology in which the researcher's own experience becomes data, subjected to the same analytical scrutiny applied to any other source. Autoethnography does not claim objectivity. It claims something more honest, that the researcher's position inside the phenomena they study is itself revealing, and examining it rigorously produces insight that purely external analysis rarely finds. We implicate ourselves in these pages because the work required it, and because a book asking dispatchers to examine their own reflexes has an obligation to model that examination rather than simply demand it.

We also sought the knowledge of our contributing writers to help inform this book. Police Chief Allen Hill offers his decades of experience and wisdom to inform these chapters. His contributions extend beyond his written components scattered throughout the book. Lieutenant Mike Valencia's contributions exemplify the importance of dispatch work and how dispatchers perform an important service to the community, even if unrecognized. Both law enforcement officers informed my Human Rights Policing training class and the books that followed.

The case scenarios in Chapter 5 are illustrative composites. They draw from documented patterns in emergency communication research, practitioner accounts, and the authors' direct professional experience, but they are not transcripts of specific calls. They are constructed to demonstrate how the principles developed across the preceding chapters encounter the full complexity of dispatch work. We have tried to be transparent about it rather than allowing illustrative scenarios to pass as documentary ones.

Together, these methods reflect a deliberate choice. Human rights dispatching is not an abstract proposition. It lives in moments, in the 30 seconds between a caller's first word and a dispatcher's first response, in the language that leaves the dispatch center and arrives at someone's door. A book that addressed only the theoretical dimension of that reality would fail the people it is written for. A book that addressed only the practical dimension would fail to equip them with the analytical tools the work genuinely requires. We have tried to write both books at once. That is the only version of this book worth writing.

Who This Book Is for

This book discusses how dispatchers can apply human rights to their work, mainly, to protect the human rights of the caller, the called upon, and the one who responds to the call. It is written for dispatchers and emergency communicators, for the people who answer the phone when someone runs out of options and reaches for the only number still available. It is also written for the supervisors, trainers, and administrators who impact the environments those dispatchers work inside, and for the scholars and students whose work touches emergency communication, policing, human rights, and the sociology of institutions. It is written, finally, for anyone who wants to understand what happens in the space between a call for help and the help that arrives, and why that space is one of the most consequential and least examined sites of human rights practice in contemporary public life.

The book makes demands. It asks dispatchers to examine assumptions they may not know they hold. It asks institutions to account for what they have long been content to ignore. It asks readers to confront the authority embedded in emergency communication and to reckon with its obligations. We do not believe those demands are unreasonable. We believe they are owed to the people on the other end of the line.

The dispatcher at the center of this book is neither saint nor technician. They are a professional doing difficult work inside imperfect systems, making consequential decisions under pressure with incomplete information, working through other people's worst moments across shifts that do not pause long enough to let any of it settle. This book is for that person. It is an argument that the work they do matters more than the institutions around them have been willing to acknowledge, and that doing it well requires more than protocol can provide.

Doing it well begins with seeing the human being on the other end of the line and protecting the rights of all those involved in an emergency call. Everything in these pages asks what that kind of attention demands, and honors the dispatchers who bring it to their work every day.

Acknowledgments

The idea for this book was born at a towny bar in La Crosse, Wisconsin, the cultural heart of the Driftless region. Chief Allen Hill, who had previously taken my human rights policing course, approached me with a simple proposition: apply human rights principles to police dispatchers and emergency operators. They are, after all, the very first point of contact.

The book traveled with me. Through the great city of Bogotá and the residential neighborhoods of Cancún. Along the island of Holbox, Mexico, where I rescued a seagull named Ms. Nelly. I walked 120 kilometers along the Camino Portugués to Santiago de Compostela, spent time in A Coruña, and kept moving – through Bratislava, Slovakia; Poland; Lithuania; and Latvia, before crossing to the other side of the world to Bangkok, Penang, Langkawi, Kuala Lumpur, Chiang Mai, Pai, and the great metropolis of Tokyo.

After returning to New Orleans and tending to my lectures in Wisconsin, I set out again – Isla Mujeres, Cancún, Madrid, Sofia and Plovdiv, Bulgaria; Niš, Serbia; Skopje, North Macedonia; Thessaloniki and Athens, Greece; Jakarta, Yogyakarta, Bali, Gili Air, Gili Meno, Labuan Bajo, and Komodo National Park, Indonesia; Kanchanaburi and Sangkhla Buri, Thailand; and Lisbon to Faro, Portugal.

Back to the States and back out again. Cairo and Alexandria, where locals tend to street cats with quiet devotion. Spain and Portugal, where my father and I found an underground speakeasy in the high hills near Porto and drank our way through the wine country of the coastal country. From Lisbon, I traveled by train through Évora, Badajoz, Cáceres, and Madrid before crossing the Strait of Gibraltar to Fès and Tangier, Morocco, then on to Rome, Bucharest, and Crete, where we spent months driving the small towns and villages of that magical ancient island where the Minoans once roamed. I picked up a pint in Dublin and Howth, moved through Cork, Kinsale, Kilkenny, and Belfast. Then, unable to resist, I traveled to Santiago, Chile, and spent weeks looking at the stars in San Pedro de Atacama and the Atacama Desert before making my way through Purmamarca, Tilcara, Jujuy, Salta, Mendoza, and Buenos Aires, then across the Río de la Plata to Colonia del Sacramento and Montevideo.

I'm headed to the Camino de Santiago, The Way of Saint James, on a pilgrimage from Saint-Jean-Pied-de-Port to the Santiago de Compostela Cathedral to spread my mother's ashes along the way. I'm still shocked and devastated, and I know I will never recover. I miss you Mom.

To the non-human animals of the world, you deserve human rights more than humans.

Dr. D.G. you my brother.

Pops, we did it again. Let's keep doing some crazy shit together in this absurd world.

Sweet Pea, I am yours forever.

The last words of this book were written in New Orleans. Who dat. We dat. And I'm forever dat.

Viva Cuba libre!

Peter J. Marina – New Orleans, La. (somewhere in human time)

Student Note

As a sociology graduate, human rights policing was never a topic that came up in my coursework, until I had the opportunity to explore it in Professor Marina's class. What the course gave me was not just a new framework but a different way of seeing one I thought I already understood.

I had known that legal rights existed, that they were written into law and enforced through institutions. What I had not grasped was the difference between those rights and human rights, rights that belong to every person from birth, not because any government granted them, but because the United Nations Declaration put into writing what no law had fully stated before. These rights are universal, unconditional, and cannot be taken away. That distinction changed how I understood what law enforcement is responsible for. Officers are obligated not only to follow the law, but also to protect the humanity of every person they encounter, including people who have broken the law, including people who are in crisis, and including people whom the system has already failed.

What the course made concrete for me was how that obligation operates under pressure. Law enforcement decisions happen fast, in situations where information is incomplete, emotions are high, and the easiest path is often the one that ignores what human rights require. Training matters precisely because the moment of decision rarely allows for deliberation. Human rights practice must be built into how officers and dispatchers think before the call comes in, not afterward.

That last word, dispatchers, represents one of the course's lasting contributions to my thinking. I understood dispatch as part of the process, as a mediator between law enforcement and the caller. Professor Marina's work helped me see it as the first point of contact where human rights are either protected or abandoned. The dispatcher is a vital part of human rights implementation. They frame calls, decide how a situation is described and what officers are told to expect, and shape every encounter that follows. That is not background work. It is human rights work.

Human rights in policing is still finding its footing. But what this course taught me is that the framework is already present, in the UN's Declaration, in the scholarship, and in the approach this book develops. What remains is the will to apply it at every point in the system where one person's authority touches another person's life. – Carson Beier

Chapter 1

Human Rights

Possession Versus Experience

I walk past a man saying he is dying.

He's sitting on a downtown Philadelphia sidewalk, saying it clearly: *Help, I am having a heart attack, please call 911*. People walk past him without breaking stride. I do too.

I make it a few feet before turning around.

I ask him if he's having a heart attack. He says yes. I ask if he wants me to call an ambulance. He says yes. I call 911 and tell the dispatcher that a man who appears to be homeless is sitting on a downtown Philadelphia street between two intersections, reporting a heart attack and needing an ambulance immediately. The dispatcher tells me help is on the way and that he will be safe. I thank her and stay with him.

We talk while we wait. He has worked with his hands most of his life, a laborer of some kind, a former working man. And he's easy to talk to. After a few minutes he stops mentioning his heart and starts mentioning his hunger. By the time the ambulance arrives he admits that what he really wants is chicken soup. I tell him to keep complaining of chest pains so they admit him to the hospital and get him some. He smiles.

The paramedics step off the ambulance, look at me, look at him, and their faces tell me they had been here before, either with this man specifically or with a version of this situation they knew well. One of them thanks me, tells me to leave it with them, says they have it from here. I tell the man, without anyone else hearing, that I hope he gets his chicken soup, and walk away.

It's the few feet I walked past him that stays with me. That distance is small in physical terms and immeasurable in human ones. I heard a man say he was dying and kept walking, holding the reflex of indifference built over years of growing up in New Orleans and living in New York. Simmel called this the blasé attitude, or the protective indifference urban dwellers develop against the constant assault of external stimuli (Simmel 1903/2002). In that moment it moved from a concept I studied into a reflex I enacted. I caught myself and turned around.

DOI: 10.4324/9781003583868-1

Human Rights in Action: Bobby the Firefighter

My friend Bobby is a firefighter in New Orleans. I have watched him demonstrate, both on and off duty, what human rights protection looks like at the ground level.

On one ordinary weekday night on Bienville Street just off Bourbon Street, after I finish my bartending shift at Café Beignet while conducting research for my book *Down and Out in New Orleans* (Marina 2017), Bobby and I come across a homeless Black man lying unconscious near the roadway, his body angled into the path of passing traffic, his head protruding from between parked cars. Bobby has been keeping me company during my shift and is off duty, acting as a private citizen.

I register what is in front of us and feel the familiar pull to keep moving, the same impulse I had on a Philadelphia sidewalk. Bobby registers something different. He steps in immediately, moving toward the man, assessing the situation, and acting.

He treats vulnerability as the only important fact. I stand beside him as he checks breathing and vital signs, aware that nothing about this will be documented or reframed as heroism or principle. He simply responds, secures the man, and returns to the night.

This moment stays with me precisely because it is ordinary. Human rights protection rarely comes labeled as such. I see it emerge when someone recognizes a person in need, a life to protect, and acts on what they see. Bobby does not catch himself the way I did on that Philadelphia sidewalk. He never starts walking past.

I have stood on that sidewalk. I know how easy it is to keep moving. Dispatchers face this same moment dozens of times each shift while seated at a dispatch center. The blasé attitude seeps into the dispatcher's console the same way it seeped into me on that Philadelphia street. The question is always the same: Do you keep walking, or do you stop?

Dispatch is the first interpretive act in an unfolding event. The questions a dispatcher prioritizes, the tone a dispatcher sustains, the details a dispatcher records, and the response level a dispatcher assigns influence how responders understand what's going on before getting there. Dispatchers generate the first official narrative of the crisis that holds institutional authority. How a dispatcher frames a call, as credible or suspect, vulnerable or volatile, colors everything that happens next. The dispatcher also frames the subject of the call, the person officers move toward, before that person says a word. The ability to protect everyone's human rights involved in an emergency call to dispatch demands the same conscious attention that Bobby brought to a sidewalk on Bienville Street.

The Unsung First Responder

Lieutenant Mike Valencia (Ret.) worked for the La Crosse County Sheriff's Office for 28 years, retiring as a lieutenant in investigations. He held various positions as jail officer, patrol officer, training officer, and supervisor of patrol and investigations. He was also a member and team leader of his department's SWAT team. In addition, he is a certified trainer by the Wisconsin Department of Justice. He spent many of those years on the other side of the radio, and what he saw there never left him.

> In my time as a law enforcement officer, I was able to work with some exemplary first responders who made a difference in my career. These people were always at the tip of the spear, 24 hours a day, 7 days a week. In some cases, I got awards for the ways in which calls were handled, yet there were others who literally put the "first" in "first responder" on those calls who received no credit at all. These are the unsung heroes who staff our 911 and emergency dispatch centers (EDC) across the country.
>
> Imagine a time of day in which you think something of an "emergency" could happen. Think about the early morning traffic commute into work and a serious car crash occurs. Think about a call where a voice in the house next door is screaming for help. Think about being awakened at 2AM, hearing something in your home that shouldn't be there. All of these are typical situations which prompt a 911 call to an EDC. When these calls come in, a flurry of activity initiates.
>
> A call for a serious traffic crash alone prompts several actions: notifying police for investigation, dispatching fire / rescue personnel and ambulances for patient management and scene stabilization. Often there are ancillary dispatching of other resourcing as well such as street or highway department personnel for protective signage or roadway mitigation to ensure safe passage of society going about its business.
>
> Yet, the dispatcher who takes that call is not only accomplishing these tasks but taking other calls and gathering pertinent information from witnesses, victims, or others who may be reporting the incident from their perspective. The dispatcher is running registration information, driver and passenger license status information, criminal information if it is appropriate, and other information that may be requested by responding personnel. And all the while they may also be taking additional emergency calls in the middle of the call that they are in.
>
> The EDC dispatcher is many times intimately connected to these calls yet totally disconnected from it. They are the "first" person who is responding to a critical incident yet is the one who is regularly and routinely left out when the dust settles and everyone pats themselves on the back for

a job well done. The EDC dispatcher deserves much of the credit ensuring that an emergency situation is handled promptly and professionally.

Hearing Before Seeing: The Unique Role of Dispatchers

Officers on the street see what is happening. Dispatchers hear it. Calls arrive in fragments that require interpretation under pressure. A dispatcher constructs a situation from those pieces, makes rapid decisions with real consequences, and moves immediately to the next call, listening to panicked, angry, or confused sounds. The work happens entirely through sound, through words, tone, silence, and background noise that sometimes reveals more than what the caller says.

The voice-only environment removes the visual cues that often introduce bias in face-to-face encounters. Dispatchers hear what officers cannot see. Fear appears in a trembling voice. Pain hides underneath anger. Hesitation signals uncertainty or hope. Officers read faces, posture, and clothing. Dispatchers listen to the unguarded moment of a person's experience.

This access gives dispatchers distinct authority. In seconds, they can make someone feel seen, guide a panicked exchange toward a more soothing calm, and prepare responding officers to reduce the risk of rights violations before they arrive. The way a dispatcher frames a call impacts both what the caller experiences and how the person on the other end experiences the officer who shows up. Listening carefully to both what is said and unsaid lets dispatchers influence outcomes that can't be undone.

Dispatchers who meet this challenge cultivate deep listening, remain present to every detail, anticipate the rights of both caller and subject, and hold both in mind while the queue grows and the shift continues. They already have the power to make a difference in every call, but wielding it consistently requires focus and intention. Sociological awareness, empathy, and human rights principles make explicit the moral imperative that this work involves and clarifies the quiet decisions that repeat dozens of times every shift.

Every call gives a dispatcher the chance to determine whether the people on the line experience their rights or experience them as a promise the system failed to deliver. These pages sharpen that discipline and give it structure strong enough to hold across a long career.

What Are Human Rights?

Dispatchers work at the point where legal obligation ends and human judgment begins. Civil rights protection is a duty the law defines and protocol fulfills. Human rights protection is what the dispatcher builds beyond that, in the questions asked, the tone held, and the attention brought to what the caller needs. Governments create and define civil rights. Legislatures write them into law. Courts interpret them. Officials enforce them, however unevenly. They change with politics, jurisdiction, and power. Depending on where the political winds blow, they can expand, contract, or disappear. Their existence depends on fickle institutions of authority, and their enforcement remains even less reliable.

Human rights operate differently.

Their modern articulation appears in the Universal Declaration of Human Rights, adopted by the United Nations in 1948, and in later international agreements that affirm dignity, equality, security, and freedom from discrimination as universal (United Nations 1948; United Nations General Assembly 1966). Governments do not create these rights and can't take them away. They belong to every person, everywhere, all the time, and without condition. They exist before the state and remain whether the state recognizes them or not. More precisely, all human beings, regardless of their behavior or character, possess human rights simply because they are human and these rights cannot be taken away under any circumstances.

What changes is not the right, but whether it is honored.

The difference between possessing rights and receiving them becomes most visible in emergency communication. A person can hold every human right in principle and still be denied them in practice (Donnelly 2013). In a single call, a dispatcher's response can uphold those rights or fail to deliver them.

A person calling 911 during a mental health crisis holds the right to respect, safety, and freedom from degrading treatment. A dispatcher who responds with impatience, dismisses the caller as irrational, or frames the person in crisis as a threat leaves those rights theoretical. A dispatcher who listens attentively, gathers relevant information, identifies appropriate mental health support, and conveys the situation in neutral, professional language turns those rights into practice. The rights themselves remain unchanged. The dispatcher determines whether they become real in practice.

When a sex worker reports an assault, she holds the same right to safety and protection as any other victim. A dispatcher who responds with moral judgment or dismissive framing undermines her access to justice and human rights protections. A dispatcher who treats her report as legitimate affirms her status as a rights-bearing person and enables that protection to function in practice.

Picture the person experiencing homelessness who calls 911 after someone threatens them or puts their hands on them. They call from a corner or a doorway, possibly without a fixed address to give, possibly known to local officers in ways that haven't always worked in their favor. Courts, legislatures, and local officials may apply civil protections inconsistently depending on the jurisdiction and the political climate. None of that impacts their human rights. They possess the right to liberty, security, dignity, the right to freedom from degrading treatment, the right to equal protection, and no ordinance eliminates those rights regardless of what it does to their civil ones.

When that call reaches the dispatcher, the dispatcher either affirms those human rights in practice or allows indifference, prior assumptions, and institutional habits to shove those rights aside. While the law defines the boundaries of enforcement, the dispatcher impacts how those boundaries are applied in relation to human rights in practice. Dispatchers who recognize their power in upholding human rights are better positioned to protect them, those who remain oblivious, let them dissolve into the cold, sterile, bureaucratized routine of the work.

Many of the decisions dispatchers make determine if the caller experiences the human rights they already possess. When safety is at risk, the right to life and security of person is on the line with the caller. Categorizing and prioritizing calls brings the prohibition on discrimination and the guarantee of equal protection into play, requiring decisions grounded in what's happening. When harm is reported, the right to an effective remedy belongs to the caller and to the person the call concerns. What dispatchers record, share, and escalate affects the right to privacy. Dispatchers are the first point of contact that sets the tone for what happens next. And what happens next decides the fate of human rights for all involved in the call.

Human Rights Beyond Civil Rights and Kindness

Emergency communicators already understand civil rights obligations. They know departmental policies, procedures, and standards and bring them into every call. Few, if any, dispatchers receive training in human rights dispatching. The human rights approach demands more than civil rights or attention to dignity and respect. It requires the capacity to see the world from inside another person's experience, to feel the heaviness of their situation, and to want the person on that line and the person that call is heading toward to be treated the way you would want to be treated, or the way you want your loved ones treated. Police dispatchers require professional discipline that serves the public, fellow human beings navigating the complexities and contradictions of our social world, who need human rights protections in their most vulnerable moments. This book shows how dispatchers can become the unspoken heroes defending the human rights of the people when they need them most.

The sociological imagination provides the most rigorous foundation for practicing human rights. Durkheim argues that social facts are things

(Durkheim 1982). Social facts are the institutions – political, economic, social, cultural, religious – that people inherit and rarely stop to question. We created them, but they do not behave as if we did. They impose themselves on individuals with a force that shapes behavior, constrains possibility, and in the most powerful cases, determines the conditions of an entire life. Callers on the other end of the line inherited institutions they had no hand in designing.

The root causes of social problems lie in the institutional arrangements of society. When institutions fail, people suffer. That suffering reflects structural breakdown, something broken in the political, economic, social, and cultural frameworks people inherit and navigate without choosing. Durkheim's concept of social facts as things gives dispatchers a framework for understanding human suffering without directing blame at the individual. The dispatcher who grasps this understands that the conditions producing that call run deeper than any individual.

Weber takes us the rest of the way. Structural explanation describes the conditions that produce a call, but it does not explain how those conditions appear to the caller. Verstehen requires disciplined attention to the actor's point of view. It focuses on how a person interprets what happens, what pressures they face, and what choices they have available. It also requires recognition that poverty, exclusion, marginalization, and inequality restrict those choices long before the call reaches a dispatch center (Weber 1922/1978). We do not need to approve of what we encounter. But we do need to understand how the person reporting it understands the situation.

Durkheim removes the impulse to blame the individual for social problems. Weber replaces it with the capacity to understand the perspectives of people dealing with them. Together they produce something the dispatcher can use, a way of approaching every call that is neither sentimental nor indifferent, but disciplined, clear-eyed, and fully human. Together they form what this book calls the golden rule imperative, the disciplined commitment to treating others as we would want our own loved ones treated.

When people begin from unequal positions, identical treatment produces unequal outcomes. Institutions that ignore this avoid confronting the consequences of their own practices (Donnelly 2013). Every caller, and every person the call concerns, comes from very different social conditions. Some learn to expect very little from the law enforcement agencies they call. Others with more privilege expect law enforcement to automatically defend them regardless of the situation. Treating people identically reinforces social disparities. Fairness, on the other hand, requires responding uniquely to each person understanding the context of their situation as it unfolds.

Every call is a decision about whether human rights remain a promise or become real. Tone, listening, call categorization, and subsequent decisions turn those rights into reality. The officer arrives holding a picture of who is behind the door. The dispatcher creates that picture before the officer leaves the building. Those choices impact the rights of two people at once, the caller and the person who never had the chance to speak. Communicating from a human rights perspective requires staying conscious of how power operates in these moments and acting in ways that preserve human rights, even inside systems that make it difficult.

Policy manuals and training curricula do not draw this line. Dispatchers do, call after call, through choices no performance metric fully captures.

Human Rights and Police Dispatcher Legitimacy

Bobby never read a word of procedural justice research or human rights training. Decades of research show that how people are treated often outweighs the outcome, though both count. When law enforcement, including emergency communication centers, engage people with fairness, dignity, and respect, they establish legitimacy. When interactions turn dismissive or discriminatory, legitimacy erodes, even when every procedure is properly executed.

Tom Tyler shows that public cooperation rests less on the threat of sanction than on the experience of fairness and respect (Tyler 1990/2006). People comply because they see the system as legitimate. That legitimacy forms in individual interactions beyond policy statements and statistics. I have seen it unfold riding with officers who took my human rights policing course across Wisconsin and neighboring states. Legitimacy, like respect and trust, is earned through behavior.

Professional practice shows up in the smallest moments. It's in the dispatcher who asks one steady question instead of several at once, who lets a brief silence hang so the caller can gather themselves, and who explains things in plain language.

Tyler (2003) identifies four elements that shape how people experience authority. Voice gives people the chance to tell their side before other people make decisions about them. Neutrality grounds decisions in facts. Respect honors people's dignity throughout the interaction, particularly when they are upset, frightened, or hard to reach. Trustworthiness tells the people it serves that the institution cares about them beyond the outcome it wants. These don't require *feeling* differently. They require *acting* differently.

Procedural justice explains how fairness influences the way people perceive authority as legitimate. A human rights framework establishes what people deserve, unconditionally, whether they comply, trust, or cooperate. In emergency communication, these two traditions often arrive at the same place, though they travel different paths. Procedural justice asks how legitimacy takes root and holds. Human rights declare what people deserve before legitimacy becomes a question at all.

These dynamics take on greater force in communities with long histories of distrust (Tyler and Huo 2002). Communities that have endured sustained mistreatment at the hands of law enforcement bring that history into every call. Dispatchers work within a system that helps create those conditions. Research on police–minority relations shows how distrust concentrates in places where negative encounters accumulate over time (Tyler and Huo 2002). Each negative interaction adds to that accumulation.

Dispatchers may not see that history directly, yet callers reveal it in hesitation, in guarded phrasing, and in their surprise when a dispatcher's tone signals care and attention. Black residents experience higher rates of stops, use of force, and fatal encounters than white residents, with research linking these disparities to racial bias across multiple stages of the system (Dovidio and Solomon 2025). Dispatchers operate within the infrastructure that sustains these disparities.

How dispatchers listen, question, and respond determines if callers meet an institution that recognizes their humanity or one that reduces them to cases to manage. That encounter builds across a lifetime of interactions with systems never designed with equal regard in mind. A single call carries that accumulated history and the chance to answer it differently.

Case Vignette

The call comes in at 2:14 a.m. A woman speaks in a controlled voice that falters just enough to notice. She spent nearly an hour building the courage to call. She says her neighbor keeps yelling. She pauses and then apologizes. That apology contains more meaning than the words surrounding it. It tells you everything about what she expects from the agency she just reached out to and what she fears it will do with her concern. She worries she will be dismissed before finishing her first sentence.

She hands you two lives. Herself, the caller on the line, and the neighbor behind the wall who will never speak to you, but whose safety depends entirely on what you do next.

One dispatcher hears a woman and handles the call efficiently. The questions come fast and land flat. When the caller's voice tightens and she starts to explain what happened last week, the last month, the last time she heard that sound through the wall, the dispatcher talks over her to confirm the street address. The call gets coded. An officer gets dispatched. The line goes dead in under two minutes. Every box got checked. Nothing got heard. The caller sits in the dark holding a phone that just taught her something she will not forget. Her fear was an inconvenience. Her neighbor was an address. The officer pulls up to a door with a number and nothing else, no voice, no history, no human being waiting on the other side of it.

Another dispatcher hears the same trembling voice and does something different. When the caller apologizes for calling, the dispatcher tells her she did exactly the right thing. The questions have purpose and patience. When the caller's voice tightens and she reaches back into what's been building for weeks, the dispatcher stays with her and listens without interruption. Then the dispatcher asks questions that clarify the situation and explains their purpose. The tone never wavers. By the time the call ends, the caller knows something important. She was worth the call. She was worth the time. The officer leaves the building with more than an address. He holds a person in mind, a human situation, and a set of details that will impact the moment he knocks on that door.

The formal outcome is identical. No arrest. No report distinguishes one call from the other. The difference exists entirely in the experience of the people involved. The caller hangs up feeling heard. That feeling decides if she calls again the next time danger finds her or faces it alone. The neighbor behind the wall feels the difference the moment the officer knocks, whether the officer is prepared to meet a human being in distress or to manage an inconvenient address during a long shift.

Every choice a dispatcher makes says something important. Allowing a caller to finish a sentence tells her she is heard. Explaining why a question is asked tells her she deserves to understand what is happening. Staying present throughout the call tells her she contacted someone who takes her seriously.

The Power of First Contact: Evidence From Training

After growing up in a police family in New Orleans and living in New York City, working as a public school teacher at the Crossroads Juvenile Detention Center in Brownsville, Brooklyn, I wanted to know what makes cops tick in small town middle America. I conducted ride-alongs with officers in the La Crosse Police Department and La Crosse County Sheriff's Department in Wisconsin, spending hours in squad cars talking about life and work while driving city and county roads. Police officers don't always trust academics, and for good reason. Academics often write about people, telling their stories for them, making theories that explain people without ever knowing anything about them or their communities. I have always believed in the ethnographic approach, using your body as a tool to acquire knowledge, immersing yourself in the world of others to learn about human social reality from direct and intimate experience. The cops and I got along, and maybe that was inevitable. Perhaps it was my police blood. I grew up riding in unmarked cars through the roughest neighborhoods in New Orleans while my father stayed hidden, sending me to knock on the doors of his drug informants and walk them back to wherever he was waiting, because a kid drawing no attention was better cover than any badge. That was my first foray into becoming an ethnographer. Or perhaps I got along with cops because of the rougher edge that comes from growing up in an immigrant family in the working-class Gentilly neighborhood of New Orleans. During those ride-alongs in Wisconsin, I met a sergeant (later lieutenant) named Mike Valencia

Mike Valencia immediately impressed me. We were riding the city and rural streets of La Crosse County when a call came in. A girl of about 17 detained at a county mental health facility was having a crisis. Valencia took the call, and we headed to the scene. Upon arrival, we met Vanessa, a young woman in clear distress. Valencia showed compassion immediately, speaking in a gentle, unhurried voice with no assertion of authority, no cop-speak, nothing bureaucratic or formal. He asked questions like a skilled ethnographer, open-ended questions that elicit stories and give voice to people who want to tell them, without a hint of judgment or condescension. She felt heard. She felt like someone cared. Another officer might have resolved the situation efficiently and moved on. Not Valencia. He sat with her patiently, eye to eye, while she talked through her struggles. He even advocated for her to go outside for a smoke. By the time they were done, the crisis had passed and no one got arrested. Valencia practiced human rights policing without knowing it.

Over several years, my father and I delivered human rights training to law enforcement officers across Wisconsin and neighboring states. Officers consistently reported that learning human rights principles and the sociological imagination changed how they engaged people in the community. Officers described moving from seeing individuals only through offense categories to recognizing the structural contexts shaping behavior. This shift sharpened their work and broadened their understanding of policing. Understanding how poverty, trauma, and systemic inequality impact the behaviors they encounter made officers feel more professionally grounded. Respecting human rights became a discipline that made decisions more precise and their work more deliberate and meaningful.

Sergeant Andrew Hyatt of the Wisconsin State Capitol Police Department took the course shortly after the unrest following George Floyd's death. He entered skeptical, concerned the training might be anti-police or politically slanted. He left with two lessons he could not set aside. The first was the Universal Declaration of Human Rights and what it demands in daily work. People hold rights into every encounter that no arrest, ordinance, or difficult night can erase. The second was human agency, the recognition that an officer can act differently than institutional habit dictates and make a difference regardless of the choices their colleagues make. He thought of the homeless person an officer might pass off as too complicated or too time-consuming. He said that human agency reaffirmed something he already believed. Policing at its best helps people.

What stayed with him most was storytelling. The course sent police officers into the communities they serve to better understand the people within them. Officers listened to residents' stories and shared their own. Sergeant Hyatt returned transformed. Hearing those stories, he said, humanized the people he met.

Another officer described a traffic stop that I have never forgotten. He pulled over a woman who looked worn through, with an old car, frayed clothes, and the kind of exhaustion that had nothing to do with the hour. A baby rode in the back seat without a car seat. His training pointed toward a ticket. Then something shifted. He found himself thinking of Weber's verstehen, the capacity to see the world through another person's eyes and understand what it costs them. He began to think sociologically, to see how poverty shapes the conditions of a life no individual fully chooses, and few easily escape. The woman in front of him had no margin for a mistake, let alone a ticket. He set aside the ticket and bought a baby seat.

Lieutenant Valencia recalls a different kind of stop. On a late patrol, he stopped a motorcycle after clocking it speeding, and when the passenger fell into the grass, he recognized immediately that they both were intoxicated. He arrested the driver and drove him to jail. On the way, the man mentioned he was traveling to speak about post-traumatic stress disorder (PTSD). When Valencia asked how he came to that work, the man said his family had been killed by a serial killer. Then he went silent. Valencia booked him, gave him his card, and told him to call if he ever needed anything. He later learned the man was indeed a documented victim of a serial killer's violence. What stayed with Valencia was not the arrest. It was the silence after the man spoke, and the question he has returned to since. He wonders if should have paused, asked a different question, or had his dispatcher pull background in that moment that might have changed his decision to arrest the man. He did his job. But he has never stopped wondering if he could have done something more. That wondering came without training to name it, which is exactly what this chapter is about.

The training produced a sharper officer capable of seeing the whole person beyond their immediate legal violation. Institutions slowly build into people the tendency to cite and move on. Human rights training gives officers the capacity to pause inside that tendency and ask what the situation requires.

Dispatchers stand to gain even more from these transformations than officers. Officers engage after situations escalate. Dispatchers engage at first contact, before anyone reaches the scene and before narratives harden into fact. They frame the questions, set the tone, and determine what responding officers know before they arrive at the scene. How encounters begin rests with them at the start of the call, affecting both the caller and the person the call is directed toward.

The sociological imagination equips dispatchers to interpret calls with a precision beyond protocol. It helps them recognize when a suspicious person's report reflects caller bias while actual conduct tells a different story, when a mental health crisis requires careful framing, and when repeated calls indicate unmet needs within a community. Dispatchers stand at the front of the justice process, and the first point of contact where human rights protections begin.

The Three Types of Human Rights Communication Interactions

The three interaction types discussed later build on work developed in *Human Rights Policing* (Marina and Marina 2023), adapted here to the dispatcher's console. The dispatcher may seem peripheral in institutional descriptions, but in practice, human rights protection begins before any officer steps out the door.

Jack Donnelly identifies three patterns in how duty-bearers and right-holders interact in the protection of human rights (Donnelly 2013). Adapted to emergency communications, these patterns illuminate how dispatchers exercise authority and how rights are realized, restricted, or quietly ignored in a single call.

Assertive Exercise Interactions

In an assertive exercise interaction, a caller raises a concern tied to a human right. The dispatcher responds within the limits of policy, safety, and available resources. Even routine decisions are never neutral.

A parent calls and asks that officers enter calmly because their child has autism and will panic at the sight of drawn weapons. The parent asserts the child's right to dignity and safety. The dispatcher can dismiss the request, respond defensively, or treat it as operationally relevant. A human rights-centered response takes the concern seriously, incorporates it into decision-making, and ensures officers make it to the unfolding scene with the context they need to reduce unnecessary escalation. The dispatcher asks what usually helps when the child becomes upset and commits to relaying that to responding officers. No promise is made about tactical outcomes. The parent's knowledge of their own child is treated as information, not inconvenience.

A domestic violence victim whispers that she wants no sirens because her abuser will know she called. In that whisper lives a claim. She asserts a right to safety that extends beyond the immediate moment into the hours after officers leave. The dispatcher weighs the request against urgency and officer safety, but begins by treating it as legitimate.

Active Respect Interactions

Active respect occurs when the dispatcher recognizes rights at stake without the caller ever naming them. Responsibility shifts from the caller asserting rights to the dispatcher anticipating and protecting them. Active respect demands more than assertive exercise because it requires reading what remains unsaid as carefully as what is spoken.

A domestic violence caller whispers and sounds afraid. She makes no specific request, yet a dispatcher who hears the fear shifts to yes-or-no questions, keeps the line open, and coordinates a quieter response when the situation allows. An elderly caller speaks slowly, appears confused, and struggles to explain what is wrong. He invokes no right to dignity or patience, yet the dispatcher who slows down, simplifies questions, and weighs a medical response against a law enforcement one protects those rights through attentiveness alone.

The caller who most needs protection is often the least able to ask for it. The dispatcher must act on what they infer from silence, from hesitation, from a voice that says what words cannot. This discipline moves beyond minimal compliance. Humanity deserves protection regardless of the ability to demand it.

Objective Enjoyment Interactions

Dispatchers achieve objective enjoyment interactions when they realize rights so seamlessly that neither the caller nor the dispatcher frames the exchange in rights language. Rather than being invoked, claimed, or consciously applied, human rights live inside every word, pause, and decision the dispatcher makes without naming them.

A man calls at three in the morning. He has been sitting alone with whatever drove him to the phone for hours. The solitude drains his voice to a flatness the dispatcher immediately hears. He chooses his words carefully, as though each one costs something, still unsure if it will be enough. He never asks for patience or to be taken seriously. He simply speaks, slowly, into the dark. The dispatcher hears what's beneath the careful words, the fatigue in his voice, and stays with him through the pauses and break in his words and sentences. She asks one more question, the one nobody wrote down, the one that goes beyond the guarded version of the story into the real one. The right help heads toward him. The call ends. She takes the next one.

Nothing in that exchange announced itself as ethically significant. No one names any principles, claims rights, or consciously applies standards. The dispatcher hears a person and responds with sustained attention and sound judgment about what the situation requires. In strong practice, dispatchers do not stop to think in terms of human rights in the moment. They recognize what a caller needs and act on it immediately through listening, questioning, documentation, and response decisions. Over time, that practice becomes consistent enough that callers receive the protections their situation requires as routine work rather than deliberate reflection.

All three interactions ask an essential question for the dispatcher. How does discretionary authority turn abstract rights into real experiences? When dispatchers respond to explicit claims, anticipate unspoken vulnerabilities, and embed respect so deeply into routine practice that it becomes second nature, they determine whether human rights shape the moments people need them most or remain principles that policy documents claim and daily practice ignores.

Every caller possesses human rights. A highly skilled or ineffective dispatcher does not change that fact, but does determine whether callers experience those rights in practice. Every decision at the dispatch center determines the standard of treatment the caller receives.

What Training Leaves Out

Chief Allen Hill spent more than three decades moving through the institutional architecture of American law enforcement, from state trooper on Texas highways to university police chief in Wisconsin, watching how the system trains the people it places in its most consequential roles. That arc taught him what the training manuals never cover. Below, Chief Hill provides insight on the importance of dispatcher training that stems from a career built on both ends of the radio.

> What I keep coming back to is how often we train dispatchers to manage calls, but not to fully understand the people inside them. I have sat in training rooms across the country where the curriculum was heavy on protocol, call types, priority codes, liability, and compliance. All of that matters. Dispatchers need structure, and they need to know how to move quickly and accurately. But too often, the training stops there. What is missing is the deeper understanding that dispatchers are not just processing information. They are interpreting human distress, assigning meaning to uncertainty, and making decisions that can shape everything

that follows. In my view, we have not done nearly enough to teach dispatchers how to recognize trauma, desperation, fear, bias, mental illness, disability, poverty, cultural difference, or the simple reality that many people call 911 on the worst day of their lives and may not sound calm, coherent, respectful, or credible.

That matters because by the time many people dial 911, they are already overwhelmed, exhausted, humiliated, desperate, or completely out of options. Some are in crisis. Some are afraid of law enforcement. Some are afraid no one will come at all. Some are reporting a real danger, and some are reporting what turns out to be their own discomfort or prejudice. A protocol manual can tell a dispatcher what question to ask next, but it does not teach them how to hear the human being behind the answer. It does not teach them how easily frustration can sound like noncompliance, how trauma can sound like confusion, or how fear can sound like aggression. Without that understanding, dispatchers can unintentionally narrow a call too quickly, label a person too harshly, or mistake vulnerability for threat.

That is why I believe human rights dispatching belongs at the center of dispatcher training. We ask dispatchers to do extraordinarily difficult work for relatively low pay, under relentless pressure, often with inconsistent training standards depending on where they work. In some places, dispatchers are held to high standards with certification and continuing education. In others, the expectations are far less defined. Yet the authority they exercise is significant no matter what state they are in. When dispatchers are not trained to think about dignity, impartiality, restraint, and the human consequences of their words, the people on the other end of the line pay the price. Calls are framed too aggressively, distress is dismissed, and the system begins reacting to labels instead of people.

The Essential Role of Dispatchers

Dispatchers answer first in someone's worst moment. They hear from people experiencing homelessness, mental illness, domestic violence, economic precarity, and social isolation. Behind the words of the caller lives a person who picked up the phone anyway, who decided, against everything their experience may have taught them, that calling is worth the risk.

A dispatcher who understands that context does more than manage a call. They hear what it took to dial the number at all. They see what it costs someone to ask for help from a system that has failed them before.

The woman whispering on line one already knows the stakes. She is just hoping that someone on the other end sees her this time.

The Call That Doesn't Close

Not every call resolves the way the dispatcher imagined. Some close before the full truth surfaces. Lieutenant Valencia offers one more glimpse of what follows the dispatcher into the next call.

> On a not particularly quiet morning, EDC takes a 911 call regarding a spouse which may have taken their life. The dispatcher takes this call and remains on the phone to gather more information from the caller, which is critical in these cases. The dispatcher alerts other dispatchers of the need for additional resources: law enforcement for investigation, the fire department and ambulance for patient / victim management.
>
> The dispatcher who is still speaking with the caller, is assessing numerous areas – the safety of the person calling, the safety of the victim, and the safety of all those who are responding, as well as ensuring that the scene of the incident remains unchanged if possible. We all can agree that the right questions at the right time can make all the difference. And how a person responds to those questions can assist responders in their actions taken to resolve these situations. The dispatcher calmly asks information of the person, and at times, must also be direct with the person to ensure that those who are coming to help can safely do their jobs.
>
> When the responders arrive safely and make contact with the caller, the 911 dispatcher can finally take a deep breath, but only briefly. Another 911 call comes in and the process starts all over again. Other jurisdictional dispatchers remain on this call until its conclusion. The 911 dispatcher was not aware of how this call was resolved. They learn that the spouse did not take their life, rather, that life was taken by the person who called . . . the person the dispatcher talked with to gain critical information was the same person who ended another's life.

References

Donnelly, Jack. 2013. *Universal Human Rights in Theory and Practice*. 3rd ed. Ithaca, NY: Cornell University Press.

Dovidio, J. F., and P. A. Solomon. 2025. The scope of racial bias in policing: Behavioral science's role in a systemic problem. *RSF: The Russell Sage Foundation Journal of the Social Sciences* 11 (3): 22–85.

Durkheim, Émile. 1982. *The Rules of Sociological Method*. Translated by W. D. Halls. New York: Free Press.

Marina, Peter. 2017. *Down and Out in New Orleans: Transgressive Living in the Informal Economy*. New York: Columbia University Press.

Marina, Peter, and Pedro Marina. 2023. *Human Rights Policing: Reimagining Law Enforcement in the 21st Century*. New York: Routledge.

Simmel, Georg. 2002. "The Metropolis and Mental Life." In *The Blackwell City Reader*, edited by Gary Bridge and Sophie Watson, 11–19. Oxford: Wiley-Blackwell. Originally published 1903.

Tyler, Tom R. 2003. "Procedural Justice, Legitimacy, and the Effective Rule of Law." *Crime and Justice* 30: 283–357.
Tyler, Tom R. 2006. *Why People Obey the Law*. Princeton, NJ: Princeton University Press. Originally published 1990.
Tyler, Tom R., and Yuen J. Huo. 2002. *Trust in the Law: Encouraging Public Cooperation with the Police and Courts*. New York: Russell Sage Foundation.
United Nations. 1948. *Universal Declaration of Human Rights*. https://www.un.org/en/about-us/universal-declaration-of-human-rights.
United Nations General Assembly. 1966. *International Covenant on Civil and Political Rights*. United Nations Treaty Series, vol. 999, 171.
Weber, Max. 1978. *Economy and Society: An Outline of Interpretive Sociology*. Edited by Guenther Roth and Claus Wittich. Berkeley: University of California Press. Originally published 1922.

Chapter 2

Dispatchers, Dual-Subject Asymmetry, and Human Rights

You push through the door and the room registers you before you register it. Light pours from rows of monitors, sharp and unrelenting, draining faces of color and filling them with focus. Maps pulse across screens, city blocks flare and fade as calls move through the dispatch center. Voices emerge beneath it all, never loud or quiet, each one separate, intact. A whisper so controlled it shakes. A voice holding steady for someone who isn't. Two coworkers exchange four words only to return to their screens before finishing a thought.

Chairs roll forward an inch, back an inch. Fingers move across keyboards in patterns drilled past the point of thinking. A pen taps once and stops. A note gets written, circled, handed off. Coffee goes cold on the desk while more urgent business takes place. Nobody looks up for long.

Then a call comes in and the body answers before the mind does. Shoulders settle. A voice drops into something clear and exact. Questions continue one after another, stripped to what is most critical. The person calling cannot see this room, but it holds them completely. One side exposed while the other remains structured and unseen. Every answer they give narrows the next question. Every second demands a choice.

Time breaks into small units. Each one must be resolved before the next begins. You see it in the way bodies lean toward computer screens, as if proximity could collapse the miles between this room and whatever happened somewhere in the city. Someone lets out a slow breath, once, and picks up the next call.

A woman speaks just above a whisper, selecting each word carefully. The dispatcher listens, reads what the voice says beneath the words, and begins to move the call forward. Across the room, a teenager reports chest pain while a woman screams his name in the background. Another dispatcher takes it in, assigns a priority, and translates what she heard into the language officers will use when they arrive at the door. A third call rings. Someone reports a suspicious person walking through a neighborhood. The dispatcher records it, decides what's relevant, and prepares it for dispatch.

DOI: 10.4324/9781003583868-2

The dispatcher has perhaps 30 seconds to assess each call, assign a priority, frame it for the officer who will respond, and move to the next one. The people whose lives turn on these decisions will never see her face. That framing decides which units are sent, how fast they respond, and what officers expect at the scene.

Every emergency call contains a structural feature that remains largely unexamined in both scholarship and practice. The dispatcher does not engage a single subject but two: the caller who speaks and the person the call concerns, who never enters the conversation yet may bear its consequences most directly. This condition can be understood as "dual subject asymmetry" in emergency communication. One person has voice, access, and the ability to frame reality. The other is rendered through description and acted upon without ever participating in the exchange. The dispatcher stands between them, translating one person's account into a response that will land on someone who never spoke. In this exchange, two people are bound together under unequal conditions of knowledge, visibility, and control.

Understanding Dispatcher Power

Dispatcher authority operates through this dual-subject structure and requires a clearer account of how power functions in emergency communication. Max Weber defined power as the probability that one actor within a social relationship will carry out their own will despite resistance (Weber 1922/1978). In emergency communication, this plays out in how dispatchers determine whether assistance is sent, how they prioritize response levels, and how they frame the situation for responding personnel before arrival.

This power impacts both subjects in the call. The caller speaks. The subject of the call remains silent. That person cannot contest the description that will determine how others encounter them. The dispatcher translates one person's account into institutional action. In doing so, they hold the power to determine how that person will be interpreted, and therefore, how that person will be treated once an officer makes it to the scene.

A woman calls quietly while her partner stands in the next room holding a knife. A dispatcher who hears what that silence means sends help immediately. A dispatcher who treats it as a routine domestic dispute slows the response. How the situation is read decides if help comes on time.

The same process unfolds when a caller reports a suspicious person. Describing a "suspicious Black male" introduces a racial frame that can heighten a perceived threat before an officer hits the scene. A neutral description, a person walking in the area with no crime observed, communicates the same facts without adding that frame.

A teenager calls about suicidal thoughts. A dispatcher who stays on the line keeps a human connection in place. A dispatcher who clears the call quickly removes it. The headset, console, radio, and CAD system connect the dispatcher to the larger system that responds. A caller reports. The dispatcher decides what happens next.

Dispatchers use this power on every call. It works through classification, prioritization, and the way a situation is described. It impacts what happens to the person who calls and to the person who is talked about. Any effort to bring human rights into emergency communication starts here.

The Two Orientations: Warrior Dispatch Versus Guardian Dispatch

Recent policing scholars identify two different orientations toward policing that influence how law enforcement engages with the public. Officers typically adopt either a warrior or guardian mindset (Stoughton 2014). The President's Task Force on 21st Century Policing (2015) emphasized this distinction as central to improving police-community relations, noting that law enforcement culture must embrace a guardian orientation to build trust and legitimacy. This distinction was developed primarily through studies of patrol and field operations, where officer mindset directly shapes encounters with the public. The same framework applies to emergency communications. Dispatchers exercise influence over how others interpret calls, how officers perceive urgency and threat, and how they deploy resources. The orientation a dispatcher brings to each call shapes operational decisions and their human consequences (Clifton, Torres, and Hawdon, 2021; Murphy and McCarthy 2024), including consequences for people who never enter the call itself.

Two dispatchers sit at identical stations, working the same shift, receiving the same calls, trained on the same training manual, protocols, and equipment. One operates from a warrior orientation. Every call passes through suspicion, recasting the public as potential threats. Officer safety dominates every decision and crowds out everything else. When briefing a responding officer, the dispatcher primes them to adopt a defensive posture: "Be advised, the caller sounds evasive and could be setting you up." "Approach with caution, this is a high-crime area." The dispatcher labels callers as unreliable, manipulative, or unworthy of extra time, discards any context beyond immediate risk, and frames every encounter.

The second dispatcher operates from a guardian orientation. The same calls come through, but this dispatcher reads them as actions of people navigating a crisis who need assistance and hold human rights. Officer safety remains essential, but it sits alongside the rights and humanity of everyone the call impacts. When briefing a responding officer, this dispatcher delivers context: “The caller reports a family member in a mental health crisis who has responded well to a calm approach in the past.” “This is a domestic situation, the victim is safe at the moment and requests no sirens to avoid escalation.” That briefing gives the officer actionable understanding of a human situation and supports a response proportionate to what is happening, including for the individual whose situation dispatch conveys.

While both dispatchers execute identical protocols, they differ in orientation, in what rights and risks they recognize when a call comes in, and in the information they pass into the response.

The Institutional Script: Beyond the Stanford Prison Experiment

In 1971, Philip Zimbardo recruited college students for what he described as a study of prison life. He assigned some the role of guards and others prisoners, dressed them accordingly, and placed them in a simulated jail in the basement of Stanford University’s psychology building. Within days, the guards grew cruel, and the experiment ended after six days. For decades, it stood as a defining illustration of how ordinary people given power over others descend into brutality (Blum 2018; Le Texier 2019).

Contemporary scholars have made this account more nuanced. Researchers examining the original data found that Zimbardo and his team instructed the guards to be tough, to assert dominance, and to make the prisoners feel powerless (Le Texier 2019; Blum 2018). The participants followed a script they understood the situation required.

This reading shifts the problem. Institutional hierarchy produces abuse as a function of its design. It relies on power and coercion built into its structure. Scripts cultivate cruelty by making it feel normal. They routinize control, shaping perception and behavior until compliance feels like simply doing the job. This logic extends into institutional systems where procedure replaces judgment and action becomes detached from consequence.

Hannah Arendt observed this at its most extreme during the trial of Adolf Eichmann, an architect of mass murder who acted through disciplined compliance to a bureaucratic institution (Arendt 1963). Arendt’s warning is direct. The most dangerous institutional actor is the one who stops thinking.

Eichmann depended on routine while functioning in a rationalistic bureaucracy. He followed procedure without regard for what it produced. He reduced people to abstractions. He framed his actions as simply doing his job.

A dispatcher who runs on autopilot is no Eichmann. But the mechanism Arendt identified operates anywhere people exercise power inside institutions, whether it be professors, administrators, low and middle level managers, or any other institutional role. Emergency communication is no exception. The dispatcher who stops asking what is happening to the person on the line, who simply processes calls, who merely follows the script because it has become the job, has stopped thinking.

A workplace culture that prizes the warrior mindset produces dispatchers who internalize it over time. When performance reviews reward speed and ignore human rights, when supervisors praise efficiency over judgment, when experienced dispatchers model detachment as professionalism, those priorities settle into daily practice. They influence how dispatchers handle calls, how they hear callers, and how others see people in crisis.

Human Agency: The Dispatcher's Path Forward

Call comes in
Voice shaking
Pieces missing

The script is already moving
Tells you what this is
Tells you who they are
Tells you how it ends before it begins

Wrong block
Wrong sound in the voice
Wrong kind of trouble

Stay in it long enough and you stop hearing people
Just codes. Just types. Just another one in the queue

Finger on the key
Units on the way
Next call lighting up

Then one night you don't ride it
You let the voice come through
You ask one more question, the one nobody wrote down

Something shifts
Not visibly. But decisively

The script slips
And for a beat, you are back
Not processing a queue
But holding a life that reaches your console and
finding someone still paying attention.

Every communications center runs on scripts. Some are written. Others pass from one dispatcher to the next until they become treated as fact. This is how calls go, clear it and move on. Scripts limit perception, narrow decisions, and make outcomes feel automatic even when the human cost is high.

A call comes in and the dispatcher pulls up the screen. The call-taker template opens. An address populates the top line, automatically pulled from caller ID or radio entry. The dispatcher listens to the voice on the line and makes an immediate assessment of the caller's reliability based on the tone, clarity, hesitation, background noise of the call before any details are fully stated. The dispatcher assigns a label in the system determining how the call is queued and prioritized. The dispatcher enters the caller into a category. By the time the dispatcher transmits the information, the framing determines what responding officers expect to find.

Agency begins the moment the dispatcher recognizes the script as nothing but guidelines and goes beyond it. A pause before assigning a label. A choice to ask one more question. A decision to hear the person instead of the pattern. These moments mark the point where procedure collides with human rights and a choice becomes possible.

Agency is the capacity to act deliberately beyond what institutional procedure demands, grounded in the recognition that the person on the line holds rights that procedure alone cannot protect. It requires active resistance to the pull of the script, call by call and shift by shift. A dispatcher who recognizes that capacity can act on it, but recognition alone is not enough. Institutional forces reinforce trained instincts at every step, which means sustaining agency demands something more than awareness. It demands the will to keep choosing it.

A dispatcher in a busy urban center gets a call from a woman she knows. Same number, same voice, fourth time this week. As the queue grows, the supervisor watches handle time. Everything about the system says end it.

But she stays anyway.

Something in the voice is off. Flat, distant, just different enough to catch her attention. She asks one more question. Is anyone else there with you? Her partner is in the next room. That extra minute changes everything.

That's agency under pressure. It is the decision to see the person instead of the pattern and to act on that recognition. Dispatchers who take this path perform the challenging work. They slow down even as speed is rewarded. They question responses that fail to fit the situation. They remain with callers who others dismiss. These moments cost time, effort, and risk, yet they define the line between obedience and the active protection of human rights.

Every dispatcher at the console faces the same institutional question. Awareness without agency is still compliance. A dispatcher can see the script clearly, feel its pull, even resent it privately, and still ride it through every call because the queue runs long and the shift grinds on and the system rewards the dispatcher who moves fast and asks nothing more. That is the more common failure. This book hopes to reach the dispatcher who refuses it.

Human rights dispatchers take a different path. They move beyond the script when it fails the person on the line. They understand the weight of what is at stake in the work and remain steady under it. They act from a clear recognition that the person on the other end of the call is a human being whose rights persist as the queue grows.

Dispatchers recognize it in the call that clears too fast, in the question left unasked, in the pause that feels wrong. They hear it in their own voice. That awareness marks a line institutions cannot erase, but the real question is what they do with it. Will they move beyond the script? Will they see the caller as a person? Will they reject the comfort of "just doing the job"? Will they claim agency? Will you?

This book is for those who recognize the capacity for human agency in themselves, for those who recognize it and are searching for the will to act on it, and for those who have never been told it has always been theirs.

Case Study: The Trayvon Martin Tragedy and Narrative Power

On the night of February 26, 2012, 17-year-old Trayvon Martin walked home from a convenience store in Sanford, Florida, carrying a bag of Skittles and a can of iced tea. George Zimmerman called 911 to report a suspicious person in the neighborhood (Hajela 2022). Trayvon Martin died less than 30 minutes later (U.S. Department of Justice 2015).

That recorded call illustrates how the power of narrative framing can determine what happens next, and to whom. Trayvon Martin lacked a say in the conversation. The words a caller chose transformed him from a teenager walking home into a perceived threat. That perception guided every action as the scene unfolded. The dispatcher could redirect Zimmerman's actions but could not pull him out of the story he had already decided was true. The outcome demonstrates how small choices in language bring irreversible consequences.

Zimmerman was no dispatcher. He was a neighborhood watch volunteer. From the opening moments of the call, Zimmerman reduced Martin to a type, "a real suspicious guy," ignoring him as a person. "These assholes they always get away" (Sanford Police Department 2012). Those words reported judgment, not observable behavior. They turned a teenager walking home in the rain into a symbol of danger. Once that framing took hold, it governed everything. The warrior narrative operated here in its most exposed form, casting a member of the public as a potential threat without any act to justify it, reducing the question of belonging to a phone call that had nowhere to go but forward.

The dispatcher did exactly the right thing. When Zimmerman confirmed he was following Martin, the dispatcher responded directly: "OK, we don't need you to do that." Zimmerman said OK. He kept walking. In his own account to investigators hours later, he explained that he continued moving through the complex to find a street address for the arriving officer. The narrative had taken hold so completely that continued pursuit felt like cooperation. No dispatcher instruction reaches inside that. The words were correct. The moment they were spoken, they had already lost.

The police interrogation recorded the night of the killing also reveals that Trayvon Martin's perspective never entered the picture. Zimmerman described a suspicious figure walking through the rain. Martin, as his friend Rachel Jeantel later testified, described a creepy man watching and following him. One of those accounts shaped the call. The other never reached the console. The investigator who later questioned Zimmerman understood this clearly enough to tell him directly that the person he followed perceived him as a threat and had every right to defend himself. That understanding came hours too late, in an interrogation room, after a kid walking home with Skittles and iced tea never made it home.

Bergen Street Brooklyn: When the Caller Decides Who Belongs

I never entered the call, had no say in it, and didn't know it existed.

I was living in Carroll Gardens, in a brownstone apartment on Bergen Street. Every week or so, a man in a small truck would drive through the neighborhood ringing a bell, the old New York City signal that the knife sharpener was here. For decades, these mobile sharpening services had been a city staple, the kind of working-class urban institution that feels ordinary until you notice it, and I always did.

One afternoon I heard the bell and decided to sharpen something, anything. Most people grab kitchen knives. I grabbed an old sword I had picked up at an antique shop in upstate New York, held it from its sheath, and walked a few blocks down Bergen Street toward the Brooklyn Inn, near where the truck usually stopped.

The sharpener looked at my sword the way a craftsman looks at something undeserving of his time. His eyes moved from the blade to me, carrying either disappointment or a careful anticipation of mine. Turns out, the sword was cheap, worth neither his time nor his skill. He handed it back without a word, only a small shake of the head. I slid it into the sheath, dropped my head in Charlie Brown fashion, and started walking back toward my apartment.

I made it half a block before a police car and a white van pulled up fast, doors opening as officers stepped out and moved toward me in a way that made it clear this was no casual stop. A moment earlier I had been running an errand. Now I was something else, something that required a response.

They asked what I was doing, and I told them the truth, that I had tried to get my sword sharpened but the sharpener had rejected it on the grounds that it was cheap and useless, which was accurate, though it sounded thin even as I said it, the kind of explanation that depends less on what happened than on what the listener has already decided about you.

Then they told me why they were here.

Someone had called 911 to report a crazy Mexican walking down the street with a sword.

I am Cuban American.

The description reached the system before I reached the corner. It became the version of me that officers acted on. By the time the officers arrived, I was already inside it, explaining myself from within a story I did not create.

They inspected the sword, one of them mentioning that he collected them, and after a brief exchange they confirmed it was legal, told me to have a good evening, and left. I walked back to my apartment holding the same cheap decorative sword, on the same street, in the same neighborhood, aware that nothing about what I had done had changed and that only the story had.

It could have gone another way. That part stays with you.

What the caller reported was not behavior so much as interpretation, a person who seemed out of place on Bergen Street with its big, beautiful Brooklyn Brownstones holding an object that, in the hands of someone already decided to be dangerous, became a weapon. The description that reached the dispatcher, a crazy Mexican with a sword, captured what the caller believed I was rather than what I was doing, and once that description entered the system, it moved forward a process.

It mobilized multiple units. It caused a confrontation on a public street. It placed me in the position of explaining myself without anyone first establishing that I had done anything illegal. I never entered that call and had no voice in it until the cars pulled up, the officers stepped out, and the afternoon became something else entirely.

By the time anyone arrives, the story is already in motion.

The call demonstrates how a narrative can mobilize a response before anyone acts in the situation. On Bergen Street, the officers arrived focused on the reality in front of them. They saw a man walking with a decorative sword and listened to a clear explanation. They guided the afternoon back to its ordinary course. A caller's interpretation traveled through the system and influenced how the people on the street appeared.

A caller decided someone was out of place, enacting the rules of de facto American apartheid. That decision traveled through the emergency communication system and mobilized a response without anyone on the receiving end having done anything to justify it. What happened after was different. The officers on Bergen Street looked at the actual situation beyond the narrative the call installed, saw a man with a cheap decorative sword and a story about a knife sharpener, and allowed me to return home. That choice, made at the scene, returned me to an ordinary afternoon. Trayvon Martin never got that moment. No officer entered the moment to set the narrative aside. The caller was already in pursuit.

Dispatchers hold the power to intervene before units roll and before anyone gets cornered on a public street the way I was on Bergen Street. A dispatcher who hears "crazy Mexican with a sword" and asks what behavior the caller observed, what concrete action rather than perceived presence generated the call, interrupts the threat narrative while it remains most open to challenge. The caller's fear is real and deserves acknowledgment. But the narrative that fear generates deserves scrutiny before it moves forward and becomes something no one can take back.

That scrutiny is the difference between a right held in principle and one enjoyed in practice. Trayvon Martin possessed every legal and moral right to walk home from a convenience store. A single phone call transformed those rights from living protections into conditional abstractions. The person walking down Bergen Street deserves to make it home as exactly what he was, a man running an errand, with his life still his own.

A Law Enforcement Officer's Reflection on Power and the Blasé Attitude

The second author, Lt. Pedro Marina (Retired), a veteran of 30 years with the New Orleans Police Department, reflects on his first homicide scene and the gradual development of what Simmel called the blasé attitude:

> At first, I did not understand it. How could a human being not be moved at the sight of a violent murder? It was such a tragedy. But to my partner, it was just another day. He was not moved.
>
> I was paralyzed at the sight. But now I am getting ahead of myself. My first homicide scene.

I was just a rookie on my first week out of police academy. On my first day, I got dressed in police attire at home to get ready for the adventure I had dreamed about for a long time. I put on my blue uniform: shirt, dark blue pants and, of course, the best part that I had been waiting for so many weeks at the academy, my gun belt. I put on my police hat, went to the mirror, and felt proud. I was now a real police officer.

So, I got in my car and drove to the Second District Police Station. Having graduated at the top of my class, I was given any district assignment I wanted. I chose the second district because it had everything: the Tulane University section, the River Bend area with so many businesses and boutiques, and, above all, some high crime areas. The area was popping.

I arrived at the district station and met with the welcoming lieutenant. He told me that I would be assigned to ride with an experienced officer who would show me the ropes. I sat for roll call, listening to the different crimes from the previous day as well as the subjects wanted for the alleged crimes. Then the best part, my new partner came to me, introduced himself, and said, 'Son, forget what they taught you at the academy, I will teach you real police work.' Well, I won't bore you with the first two days. Sure, we responded to a few burglaries, armed robberies, and purse-snatching calls, all on a code two, complete with siren and lights. Oh yes, I was the real police.

The third day was different.

At about an hour after roll call, a radio dispatch was broadcast for all district units to respond to a signal 34 – a shooting in progress. My partner looked at me, stating, 'Son, you are in for it. Tell the dispatcher that we are responding and get a description.' I got on the air to advise the dispatcher. With lights and siren, we were speeding to the intersection in question. As we were a few blocks away, my partner turned off the siren, ordering, 'Listen.' I heard gunfire, about ten shots.

My heart was speeding faster than the police car.

We arrived, guns in hand, on the scene and advised the dispatcher of our arrival while looking around. There was a man laying down on the sidewalk right at the corner. There was blood everywhere. There were also a bunch of empty casings from a semi-automatic weapon. I looked at the man, and seeing that he was still alive, I went to him, knelt down, raised his head with my hand, and asked him who had done this to him.

I'll never forget how he responded.

He said, 'Don't worry about it, I'll get him myself.' I tried to plead with him to tell me what happened, but he couldn't.

He died as I was holding his head.

I got up, looked at my hands full of blood, and walked around in a daze, unable to assimilate what I had just experienced. Then, I realized that my partner was screaming at me to get a hold of myself and advise the dispatcher to send EMS to confirm we had a homicide. I followed my partner, setting up a perimeter to protect the scene and to try to locate witnesses. Of course, there was nobody around. We stayed on the scene for about half an hour until the Homicide Unit relieved us. The platoon sergeant told us to clear the scene to remain available for the next code two.

As we got back in the car, my partner looked at me, smiling, and then said, 'Pedro, you did good. You want to get something to eat?'

I told him that right about now I could not eat. I needed some time to get over that last experience. My partner understood. He told me that he had a similar reaction when he first came on the job. But now, he said, he didn't let those experiences bother him.

I went home that night but could not sleep. I had that image in my mind. I could see this poor man as he was going through the process of dying. I went through it in my mind over and over and what I saw the moment he died was his soul, or something rising above his body, only to disappear. The body was left behind motionless and lifeless. It was many years later that I could tell my friends and my son about this experience. I was truly traumatized.

Over time, I continued to respond to many calls for service where there was much suffering. There were traffic accidents involving fatalities, family disturbances where women and children were badly hurt, child abuse, rapes, suicides, and many other tragic situations. What I noticed was that as time passed, I was more immune to the suffering. Not that I did not have empathy for those who suffered, I certainly did. But with time, I was not as affected and could quickly forget and go to the next call. I noticed the same reactions from my fellow officers. They cared about the people, but could shake off the tragedies other people experienced. Without knowing it, we eventually learned how to put each tragedy behind us and move on to the next call. There was really no other way to cope with this job and survive.

We became blasé.

Lieutenant Marina arrived there eventually, the same place his partner had reached years before him. He kept caring while surviving the job in the only way he could. Georg Simmel observed the same transformation reshaping city dwellers at the turn of the 20th century and gave it a name. In his 1903 essay *The Metropolis and Mental Life*, Simmel argued that relentless exposure to stimulation, crowds, noise, strangers, and unending distress forces people to develop a protective psychological barrier (Simmel 1903/2002). He called it the blasé attitude. Simmel emphasized that it reflects the mind's refusal to be overwhelmed. But protection comes at a cost. Over time, the barrier that shields a person from emotional overload begins to shield them from emotional reality. Officers see the tragedy. Dispatchers hear it. Voices contain terror, pain, and desperation while dispatchers remain calm, gather information, send help, and clear the line for the next call. Dispatchers develop the blasé attitude at the console just as Lieutenant Marina did on patrol.

The Girl on Atlantic Avenue

I was living in the Brooklyn neighborhood of Boerum Hill, walking down Atlantic Avenue toward the Smith Street subway, headed to Bayard Rustin Educational Complex in Chelsea where I taught high school history. It was going to be a long one. History class in the day, Sociology of Deviance at John Jay College of Criminal Justice (CUNY) in the evening, dissertation on Pentecostal tongue-speakers in Brownsville waiting for me at whatever coffee shop would have me after midnight. I was already inside the day before it started, the way you get in New York when the city moves and you move with it and stopping feels like a kind of death.

Then I heard brakes. Then a scream that I have never gotten out of my head and probably never will.

A car hit a girl. Hit her fast and hard. Her body went the way bodies go when something that size meets something that speed, and her friend, who had been walking beside her one second before, made a sound with language in it, only the part of a human being that exists prior to language, the raw animal part that knows what just happened before the mind catches up. Somewhere across the city two parents were drinking their morning coffee unaware of what the morning had already taken from them.

I noticed. I kept walking.

I thought about my lesson plan. I thought about my lecture notes. I thought about Brownsville Pentecostals and the dissertation chapter that wasn't writing itself. I went through the turnstile and onto the train and into the city and the girl on Atlantic Avenue went wherever things go when New York is loud and your life is full and there is always somewhere you have to be.

It wasn't until late that night, lying in bed in the silence after the city settled, that she came back. The body. The friend. That sound. I had walked past the worst moment of someone's life and felt almost nothing. Alone in the dark I felt everything. I'm still unsure whether what happened was grief for her or grief for what I had become. I think it was both. I *know* it was both.

I have never stopped thinking about that girl. I hope she made it. But hope isn't enough, and I know I kept walking, and those two things live in me together in a way that has never resolved.

That morning I was not a dispatcher. But I was living inside the same machinery. The demand was different. The result was the same. A human being in crisis receded into the noise of a life too full to stop, and I only found her again when the noise finally went quiet. Dispatchers rarely get that quiet. The next shift starts. The queue refills. The girl on Atlantic Avenue stays where the momentum left her.

The Blasé Attitude and Human Rights Dispatching

In *Metropolis and Mental Life*, Georg Simmel (1903/2002) shows how city dwellers build a psychological shield to survive the crush of urban life. The modern mind absorbs a relentless surge of impressions. Streets press in, faces blur, urgency never lets up. To survive, the urban dweller forms a protective filter that shields the inner self from constant assault of external stimuli. Calculation and detachment replace empathy and connection, protecting the self while reducing attention to other people's needs and presence (Simmel 1903/2002).

We see this process with greater intensity in policing. Officers move through the city entering its worst moments. Each call layers shock upon shock, and officers rely on procedure, training, classification, and command presence to manage scenes that would otherwise overwhelm them. These practices keep them effective and turn tragedy into routine. The blasé attitude shifts from survival tool to professional habit.

Dispatchers operate one step removed from the scene while holding a parallel burden. They hear the chaos without seeing it. Voices shake, scream, and break. Information arrives incomplete and urgent. They must decide, prioritize, and send help without hesitation. This discipline keeps the system functioning and saves lives while also turning crisis into a routine workload. The extraordinary becomes routine, and crisis fades into background noise.

The blasé attitude supports functioning under relentless pressure. It allows dispatchers to process high volumes of information without becoming overwhelmed. But it cannot block the protection of human rights. Each dispatcher works through a constant tension between the detachment required to manage calls and the attention required to recognize what each call demands in practice. That work happens continuously while taking calls and making decisions. It is agency in action. It appears in the ability to see people clearly, act without delay, and protect human rights while maintaining the capacity to keep the system running under pressure.

Why the Blasé Attitude Threatens Human Rights

A dispatcher in the grips of the blasé attitude stops hearing a person and starts hearing a category: the suicide call, the frequent flier, the psych run, the domestic, until the voice on the line becomes just another signal in the queue. The dispatcher loses sight of the circumstances behind each label, the intensity of the pain, and the rights the caller brings into the call, alongside the rights of the person whose situation the call will impact. Categorizing a person reduces the dispatcher's obligations, speeds the process, and substitutes scripted responses for engagement with a human situation that arrived at the console deserving better.

A mother calls about her son. He hasn't slept in four days. He told her this morning that he does not want to be here anymore. She's terrified, unsure of what to do, hoping the person who answers the phone will understand enough to send the help, the *right* help. A dispatcher who defaults to the standard response sends officers who arrive without context, without a calm approach, and without the information that makes the encounter safe for a young man in a mental health crisis. That dispatcher processed a call. A human rights dispatcher hears a mother terrified for her child and sends a response shaped by that reality, so that a young man in crisis encounters officers who arrive prepared to help rather than to subdue.

A man calls for the third time this week. The address is familiar on the screen. Dispatchers in that situation feel the pull toward labeling this caller a frequent flier and clearing the call fast. This pull makes sense given everything the shift has already demanded. Treating repeated calls as routine creates risk the blasé attitude renders invisible. The third call from the same address in a week can signal an escalating pattern of domestic violence heading toward a point of no return. A dispatcher who treats it as a nuisance misses the pattern, and the person the caller is trying to reach loses the last chance for intervention anyone will offer.

The blasé attitude produces efficiency at the cost of humanity, a trade with direct human rights consequences for two people. The dispatcher and the institution reduce people to queue entries. They prioritize speed over context and pattern recognition. They measure performance through response times and call volume while excluding the substance of the call. The human dimensions of the work get lost in what gets recorded, categorized, and ultimately ignored. This result comes directly from how emergency communication systems define success, reward speed, and treat the second person in a call as outside their scope of attention.

Dual-Subject Asymmetry in Operational Practice

Chief Allen Hill of the University of Wisconsin – La Crosse Police Department offers an account that shows how a description of a person becomes a dispatchable call. A neighbor identified him to the dispatcher as a suspicious person while he sat in his parked vehicle outside his residence. An officer responded to that report.

> It was winter, one of those Midwest nights that settles into your bones. I had only been in the city a few months, and my Texas blood was still learning what real cold felt like. I lived in a nice downtown apartment complex, and that evening I had gone out to my car to smoke a cigarette and read the news on my phone. The heater was running. The windows were up. I was doing nothing more than trying to stay warm and enjoy a quiet moment by myself.
>
> Then I noticed the squad car.
>
> It pulled in and stopped in front of me. The officer stepped out and walked toward my driver's side window. I rolled it down before he reached the door. He introduced himself calmly and professionally and asked if I owned the vehicle. I told him I did and asked if something was wrong. He said he had run the plate and knew I lived there. Another resident, he explained, had called me in as a suspicious person.
>
> That word landed with a force the officer could not have known. Suspicious. Not disorderly. Not threatening. Not trying doors, peering into windows, or prowling around cars. Just suspicious. I explained that I was sitting in my own vehicle, reading the news and smoking because it was too cold to stand outside. He nodded, apologized, and told me he was simply responding to the call. I told him I understood. He was polite, professional, and did exactly what he had been sent there to do. After a brief exchange, he thanked me, wished me well, and left.
>
> But when he drove away, the anger came fast. My ears got hot. My chest tightened. I sat there staring through the windshield thinking, who had the audacity to look at me sitting in my own car and decide I did not belong? When did existing in public become suspicious? For those few minutes, I was not a chief, not a police officer, and not someone who understood procedure and call response. I was just another person on the receiving end of someone else's fear, someone else's assumptions, and a system willing to act on those assumptions without asking enough questions first.
>
> That was the moment I understood, in a way theory alone cannot teach, how easily public authority can be set into motion against an innocent person. The officer did not create that moment, but he became the face of it. The caller's discomfort had been translated into official action. A dispatcher had taken the information, entered the call, and sent an officer. The officer, acting in good faith, made the contact he had been expected to make. No one in that chain necessarily intended harm, yet harm still occurred. I was humiliated, detained in every practical

sense of the word, and forced to absorb the message that my mere presence required explanation.

A few weeks later, I spoke with the chief of that agency. He was glad the officer had handled the situation professionally, but he also agreed that the call probably should not have resulted in a contact at all. We talked about what might prevent that kind of unnecessary encounter from happening again. The answer was not complicated, but it was important: ask better questions. What exactly is suspicious? What is the person doing? Are they trying to enter vehicles, looking into windows, hiding, trespassing, or threatening anyone? Or are they simply present in a location where someone else believes they do not belong? Those questions can mean the difference between protecting public safety and weaponizing police response for someone else's prejudice.

That shows the importance of human rights dispatching. It's not just about officer discretion in the field. It starts earlier, often with the very first person who receives the call. When a caller reports a "suspicious person," the dispatcher has a duty to do more than simply transmit the label. Human rights dispatching requires curiosity over assumption, impartiality over bias, and dignity over reflexive suspicion. If dispatchers accept vague discomfort as sufficient grounds for police intervention, then the communications center risks becoming the place where prejudice is translated into state action. In that sense, the dispatcher is not merely gathering information; the dispatcher is making a professional decision about whether the facts justify sending government power to confront another human being.

Sometimes the most important dispatch decision is not how quickly to send an officer, but whether an officer should be sent at all.

Where the System Breaks: Accountability and Dual-Subject Asymmetry

Accountability that protects human rights begins with how oversight enters dispatch work and influences judgment. Oversight arrives through supervisors who review recorded calls, quality assurance staff who score interactions, and systems that flag calls for audit after the fact. When these processes are experienced primarily as evaluative or punitive, dispatchers may orient their behavior toward what is measured and reviewable, while relying on discretionary judgment in moments that fall outside formal evaluation. This pattern reflects political scientist Michael Lipsky's argument that bureaucratic systems prioritize routinized, observable outputs as a way of managing decision-making under pressure (Lipsky 1980/2010).

The Hill incident demonstrates how procedure can remain intact while judgment disappears from the decision chain. A neighbor labeled him as suspicious while he sat in his car. The officer who responded to the report acted within procedure, as did the dispatcher. At no point in the chain was the initial label required to be interrogated before action moved forward. Harold Garfinkel's work on how institutions produce social facts through interaction rather than independent verification helps explain this dynamic. Once a label enters the system, it can come to function as a taken-for-granted reality within institutional processing, rather than remaining visible as one person's interpretation (Garfinkel 1967).

This divide between procedure and judgment determines whether accountability strengthens or weakens human rights. Emergency communication systems rely on quality assurance processes that define institutional priorities (Neusteter et al. 2019). These systems measure speed, call throughput, and procedural compliance while rarely tracking how risk develops over time or how early framing shapes later outcomes. In practice, these metrics signal what counts as success within dispatch systems, influencing operational priorities across agencies. Neusteter et al. (2019) show that 911 data systems remain fragmented across jurisdictions and are organized around broad categories such as call volume, response time, and call type, limiting the ability to assess patterns in a more granular way.

Standards that emphasize procedure without adequately accounting for judgment produce compliance. Many calls include moments where procedure cannot fully account for risk, and outcomes depend on how dispatchers exercise judgment in those situations. As Gillooly and Friedman (2026) demonstrate, rigid protocols often fail to account for the uncertainty and subjectivity of real-world calls, requiring dispatchers to rely on forms of judgment that no protocol can fully anticipate or capture.

This call reporting and response sequence consistently centers the visible subject of the call, namely the person who speaks and is recorded, while leaving the second subject, the individual described in the report but absent from the interaction, outside the scope of what quality assurance systems review and score. Dispatchers rely on the caller's account, which determines how the situation is interpreted and how responders act. This asymmetry is not explicitly captured in existing dispatch protocols but emerges from how call information is translated into categories and responses. If accountability is to serve both subjects, it must attend to how dispatchers translate spoken reports into dispatch language and how that language directs the actions of responders. Peter Manning's work on police communication shows how this translation process converts people into organizational categories that structure response decisions before arrival (Manning 1988).

Accountability That Reaches the Second Subject

Accountability that builds judgment changes how dispatchers interpret and respond to similar situations after a call fails. It traces what the dispatcher heard, what they prioritized, and what remained outside attention at the time. That process allows the dispatcher to understand how decisions are formed under pressure and adjust responses in future calls. This form of accountability protects both people involved in the call.

Every standard in call handling involves structural commitments embedded in call handling become most visible when procedure no longer fits the situation (Neusteter et al. 2019). A dispatcher who knows only procedure follows it until conditions exceed its limits. Research on dispatch decision-making shows that protocols alone cannot adequately guide action in ambiguous situations, requiring greater reliance on dispatcher judgment in practice (Gillooly and Friedman 2026).

Dispatcher wellbeing also influences what remains visible during a call. Under sustained stress and high call volume, dispatchers operate under conditions of fatigue and informational overload that make sustained attention and careful judgment more difficult in practice (Gillooly and Friedman 2026). As a result, sustained multidimensional attention becomes more difficult.

Checklists capture procedure but not the moment decisions form under uncertainty, a gap that shapes how discretion operates in practice (Lipsky 1980/2010; Gillooly and Friedman 2026). The second subject, the person described in the call but never heard, exists in what the record does not capture, processed through a system primarily built to measure only what enters it.

If accountability is to protect human rights, it must extend beyond compliance review and examine how decisions take shape under pressure. Otherwise, it records procedure while leaving decision formation outside evaluation.

The Thin Gold Line in Practice: A Dispatcher Saves Two Lives

While police officers often wear blue uniforms, dispatchers in many agencies wear gold. The thin gold line runs parallel to the thin blue line of officer mythology, but it operates from the dispatch center, where voice replaces presence and the power to protect is exercised before the first unit rolls.

The second author, Lt. Pedro Marina (Retired), reflects on the moment he understood what dispatchers do and what it costs when they do it well:

> Early in my career, shortly after graduating from the police academy and being assigned to the Second Police District, I became curious about

the voice coming through my radio, the one directing all my activities during every tour of duty. One morning, working a one-person car, I asked dispatch to carry me to headquarters on a station assignment. I took the elevator to the second floor and found the door marked Command Desk. Someone opened it, saw my uniform, and let me in. I stood there in awe, surrounded by electronic equipment, monitors everywhere, police personnel seated behind giant screens. The platoon sergeant I knew came over immediately and began explaining how the system worked. Before I headed back to the street, I asked to meet my dispatcher. He walked me to one of the consoles and introduced me to a woman whose voice I recognized the moment I heard it. I shook her hand and joked, "So you're the voice who sends me to all those crazy calls." She seemed pleased that I had taken the time to make an impersonal job personal. It did not surprise me when, days later, she called me and asked if I minded picking up a lunch she had ordered and bringing it to her at the Command Desk. I said yes without hesitating.

I mention this because years later, that same dispatcher kept me alive.

Three years after that visit, I had transferred to the Narcotics Unit. My partner and I were running surveillance from an unmarked van on a house in the Second District after a confidential informant told us he had watched a man purchase cocaine there and seen a large quantity on a table, apparently ready for distribution. Two hours into the surveillance, nothing moved. We climbed from the back of the van to the front seats to take a break. As I started the engine, a white male, roughly six foot two and two hundred and seventy-five pounds, approached the passenger side and asked if we were looking to score. My partner looked at me, read my expression, and asked what he had. He pulled two clear plastic bags of white powder from his pocket and offered them at 20 dollars apiece.

We needed to take him without telegraphing the arrest. My partner reached into her purse for two twenties to hold his attention while I came around the back of the van. She found the bills. I came around. I announced my identity, placed him under arrest, and ordered him to drop the bags and put his hands on the van.

That was when the fight started.

He looked at me and ran. I tackled him and we went down together. He got back up swinging. My partner climbed onto his back trying to bring him down. He grabbed her and threw her five feet. I charged him again and told her to get on the district channel and call for backup. She reached into the van, grabbed the radio, tuned it to the Second District channel, and screamed, "Unit 2232, 108, 108." Officer needs help.

The dispatcher cleared the channel immediately. "Unit with the 108, give me your location."

My partner screamed, "600 block of Hickory."

"All units clear and proceed."

Then the best sound I have ever heard in my life, a wave of sirens coming our way.

The dispatcher came back. "Give me a description of what you are wearing so there is no confusion on scene."

My partner answered, "My partner is wearing a black t-shirt and blue jeans. I am wearing a green blouse and blue jeans."

"10–4, 2232. All units be advised, two narcotics officers on scene, one male in a black t-shirt and blue jeans, one female in a green blouse and blue jeans."

I was on the ground with the man on top of me and my partner on his back when about two dozen uniformed officers descended on the scene. They pulled my partner clear, lifted the man, threw him several feet, and handcuffed him. My partner and I stood up covered in mud, shirts torn. One officer got on his radio. "Code four. Situation under control."

The dispatcher called our unit number. "You and Marina okay?" She had looked at the Narcotics roster and found my name. I recognized, in that moment, that this was the same dispatcher I had visited at the Command Desk three years earlier, the same one who had asked me to bring her lunch.

After we processed the arrest and finished the paperwork, my partner and I stopped at the Command Desk on our way back upstairs. I knocked, flashed my badge, and we walked in. We found her at her console. She told all units to stand by, turned to us, and said she had been worried about the two of us the whole time. She extended her hand. I said no. The three of us embraced, and I told her she had saved our lives.

She shook her head. "I was just doing my job. Officers like the two of you are the ones who save lives."

She was wrong about that, and she knew it. What she did in those seconds, clearing the channel, extracting the location, relaying our descriptions to prevent two dozen arriving officers from mistaking us for the man they were coming to stop, was the work of someone who understood that what happens at the console before officers arrive determines everything officers find when they get there. She had learned my name years before she needed it. She had taken the call personally long before the emergency made it urgent.

The Moral Compass of the Console

Dispatchers hold power that rarely announces itself. They exercise it in the ordinary texture of their work. Every word they choose or withhold, every priority code they assign, every 30 seconds they give or take from a frightened caller decides what happens after. The badge, the console, and the chain of command grant authority. The dispatcher's choices decide how that authority reaches people and whether it protects them or fails them.

A guardian-oriented dispatcher sees both people. They listen fully, consider what's important, and act to protect human rights. Their work at the console has immediate impact. That is the thin gold line where institutional power meets individual agency, where the emergency response system either shields or harms, and where two people experience the consequences of which direction it takes.

Every call challenges the human agency of the dispatcher. The blasé attitude pulls toward detachment. Institutional pressures demand speed. Bias shapes perception before judgment intervenes. Workplace culture can normalize dismissiveness until it feels like professional common sense. Against all of this, the human rights dispatcher still must see two people. Most of the time, the system makes that harder. They do it anyway.

The decisions dispatchers make go beyond manuals or training curricula. They unfold at the dispatch center, in the dark, at two in the morning, when the queue runs long and the hours drag. They happen when a terrified mother calls for guidance, when a young person teeters, when a familiar address hides a pattern no one else notices. A dispatcher listens, weighs, and acts.

References

Arendt, Hannah. 1963. *Eichmann in Jerusalem: A Report on the Banality of Evil*. New York: Viking Press.

Blum, Ben. 2018. "The Lifespan of a Lie." *GEN/Medium*, June 7, 2018. https://gen.medium.com/the-lifespan-of-a-lie-d869212b1f62.

Clifton, Stacey, Jose Torres, and James Hawdon. 2021. "Examining Guardian and Warrior Orientations across Racial and Ethnic Lines." *Journal of Police and Criminal Psychology* 36 (1): 436–49.

Garfinkel, Harold. 1967. *Studies in Ethnomethodology*. Englewood Cliffs, NJ: Prentice-Hall.

Gillooly, Jessica W., and Barry Friedman. 2026. "Rethinking Rules for 911: Dispatching Alternative Responders in Denver and San Francisco." *Criminology & Public Policy*. https://doi.org/10.1111/1745-9133.70008.

Hajela, Deepti. 2022. "Trayvon Martin, 10 Years Later: Teen's Death Changes Nation." *Associated Press*, February 24, 2022. https://apnews.com/article/Trayvon-Martin-death-10-years-later-c68f12130b2992d9c1ba31ec1a398cdd.

Le Texier, Thibault. 2019. "Debunking the Stanford Prison Experiment." *American Psychologist* 74 (7): 823–39.

Lipsky, Michael. 2010. *Street-Level Bureaucracy: Dilemmas of the Individual in Public Services*. 30th anniversary expanded ed. New York: Russell Sage Foundation. Originally published 1980.

Manning, Peter K. 1988. *Symbolic Communication: Signifying Calls and the Police Response*. Cambridge, MA: MIT Press.

Murphy, Kristina, and Molly McCarthy. 2024. "Guardian versus Warrior Cops: Predicting Officers' Support for Procedural Justice and Coercive Policing." *Policing and Society* 34 (10): 1011–30.

Neusteter, S. Rebecca, Meilynh Mapolski, Mustafa Khogali, and Megan O'Toole. 2019. *The 911 Call Processing System: A Review of the Literature as It Relates to Policing*. New York: Vera Institute of Justice.

President's Task Force on 21st Century Policing. 2015. *Final Report of the President's Task Force on 21st Century Policing*. Washington, DC: Office of Community Oriented Policing Services.

Sanford Police Department. Transcript of 911 Call. Case No. 201250001136. March 3, 2012. Sanford, FL.

Simmel, Georg. 2002. "The Metropolis and Mental Life." In *The Blackwell City Reader*, edited by Gary Bridge and Sophie Watson, 11–19. Oxford: Wiley-Blackwell. Originally published 1903.

Stoughton, Seth W. 2014. "Law Enforcement's 'Warrior' Problem." *Harvard Law Review* 128: 225–34.

U.S. Department of Justice, Office of Public Affairs. 2015. "Federal Officials Close Investigation into Death of Trayvon Martin." https://www.justice.gov/opa/pr/federal-officials-close-investigation-death-trayvon-martin.

Weber, Max. 1978. *Economy and Society: An Outline of Interpretive Sociology*. Edited by Guenther Roth and Claus Wittich. Berkeley: University of California Press. Originally published 1922.

Chapter 3

The Call Behind the Call

Seeing Beyond Your Private Orbit

It's a frigid February and the heating system is out for the 11th day. Derrick calls from a third-floor walkup apartment on Delancey Street, and the dispatch system immediately flags the address. The dispatcher recognizes it. He speaks in bursts, sentences chopped short the way cold does to breath. The dispatcher hears the anger. Beneath it is something quieter, the sound of a man who stopped expecting much. He calls the landlord, the building manager, leaves messages no one returns. He reports a dispute over heating. The queue stretches behind the call. The dispatcher can log it as a civil matter, advise him to contact housing services, and move on. But it would leave Derrick exactly where he is, in a third-floor apartment in cold February with no heat and nowhere left to call.

Every call pulls the dispatcher into a stranger's private world. Derrick occupies his apartment on the 11th day without heat, with a landlord who doesn't answer and a building manager who stopped picking up weeks ago. The people who love him can't fix it. The conditions that produce his cold apartment extend far beyond his immediate experience, going back into the command centers of political and economic power where people make decisions about housing policy, investment, zoning, and profit who will never stand in a third-floor walkup in February. Those decisions travel outward and downward until they land hard, without announcement, in the most private corners of individual lives. Derrick's trouble is immediate. The structures behind it predate him, extend past any landlord, and impact the lives of people far beyond Delancey Street.

Sociologist C. Wright Mills called this habit of mind the sociological imagination, the capacity to connect personal troubles to the public issues that produce them (Mills 1959). The sociological imagination allows us to understand how large-scale social problems impact the life of an individual. A dispatcher who lacks this imagination logs Derrick as a difficult caller, assigns a low priority code, and sends an officer to the door with the wrong

DOI: 10.4324/9781003583868-3

picture of who lives behind it. His exhaustion, repeated calls, and anger in his voice sound like a person whose institutions around him have failed consistently, leaving him with nowhere left to turn. Those institutions run deeper than a landlord. They live in housing policy, zoning, and investment that predate Derrick and will outlast him, impinging on the lives of people far beyond Delancey Street. A call on day 11 without heat is predictable, the kind of outcome failed institutions reliably produce. The dispatcher who understands this sees Derrick clearly, someone navigating inherited social conditions with the limited tools available to him, rather than a flawed character generating problems of his own making.

Most people experience structural pressure as private failures rather than a shared human experience (Mills 1959). They blame themselves for circumstances beyond any single life to control. Over time, they believe themselves solely responsible for troubles they did not cause. They become the problem. The forces that produced their circumstances go unnamed and unexamined. A dispatcher who never questions this way of thinking reads Derrick's exhaustion as belligerence, his repeated calls as a nuisance, his desperation as a character flaw. That misreading sets the priority code, the tone on the line, and the version of events the officer brings to the door.

Émile Durkheim developed the concept of anomie to explain what happens during times of rapid social transformation when the institutional norms holding life together collapse (Durkheim 1897/1951). Anomie is the feeling that the floor dropped out from under an entire life, that the landmarks disappeared, that the bonds holding a person to family, community, meaning, and future dissolve. Anomie goes beyond hardship and pain. It arrives when rapid social transformation, economic instability, and the erosion of community life loosen the moorings that once made existence coherent and bearable, leaving the individual with nothing solid to stand on. People experience anomie as a feeling of normlessness, meaninglessness, precarity, and dread.

Anomie is a constant presence of modern life, always lurking at bay. The attentive dispatcher hears it every shift. It sounds like Derrick on day 11 without heating, calling into a system that refuses to answer and shows no sign of answering. It sounds like an address that generated 15 calls this year because nothing that produced those calls found resolution. The dispatcher cannot restore what the conditions of anomie dismantled. But the dispatcher who recognizes their sound stops treating the people as the problem and starts hearing the structural conditions, that is, the institutional failures that drove them to the phone.

What previous experiences a dispatcher brings to that call, their own upbringing, their experience of housing and work and institutions, influences what they hear before Derrick completes a sentence. A dispatcher who grew up with stable housing and responsive landlords hears agitation and files it under difficult caller. A dispatcher who watched someone fight an indifferent system for months hears the same voice and recognizes the specific exhaustion of a person who tried everything else. Neither dispatcher chose their frame of reference. Both are responsible for examining it.

The Sociological Imagination and Policing

The second author, Lt. Pedro Marina (Retired), reflects on what the sociological imagination meant across 30 years with the New Orleans Police Department:

> I was 14 years old when my parents sought political asylum in the United States from Cuba. I grew up in a mostly white neighborhood, attended a segregated high school, studied sociology at the University of New Orleans, and eventually took the adventure a recruiting sergeant offered me when he asked if I wanted a job or something more. I chose the badge.
>
> What I did not know when I chose it was that I would spend the next 30 years policing communities almost completely foreign to me. I grew up knowing Cubans and white Americans. I had never seen poverty before arriving in the United States. I had almost no knowledge of Black New Orleans, especially the neighborhoods where I would spend most of my career. When I finally understood what I was doing, I felt like a mercenary. I came into those neighborhoods, cultivated informants, locked people away, and went home. The communities I policed were alien to me, and I was alien to them.
>
> Working undercover in the Tactical Unit changed that. Making arrests was easy. Understanding the people I was arresting took longer and demanded more.
>
> One woman stayed with me. I will call her Amanda. She faced three strikes under Louisiana law when she contacted me after her arrest, offering cooperation in exchange for consideration on her charges. She delivered. She also told me her story. She grew up in northern Louisiana in a home where her father abused her sexually and physically. She never finished high school. She cycled through addiction and employment and addiction again. The sex traffickers who kept bailing her out of jail were, in her telling, the only people who ever showed up for her. Amanda broke down several times during our conversations. She was not a criminal who happened to have a difficult past. She was a person the structure had failed at every turn, doing what survival required.
>
> Two brothers I cultivated as informants in the Narcotics Unit showed me the same thing from a different angle. I came to know them well enough to meet their mother, a schoolteacher who had no idea what her

sons did or who I was. I watched her navigate raising two kids alone in a segregated neighborhood where narcotics trafficking was as visible as the streetlights. I saw her sons as human beings living difficult lives and adapting for survival. That is not a comfortable thing for a narcotics officer to sit with. It is also the truth.

No matter how many people we arrested, crime remained. There was always someone to take the corner. Always someone to take the stash house. Always another homicide. We knew, after enough years, that law enforcement alone could not solve the problem. What we could do was choose how we treated the people we encountered inside it.

The sociological imagination gave me the language for what I had been watching for 30 years. Amanda's story was not about personal failure. The two brothers were not simply criminals. They were people solving structural problems the only way the structure had left available to them. Poverty, segregation, failing schools, absent fathers, no access to healthcare, and constant police pressure did not excuse their choices. It explained the conditions those choices emerged from. That distinction changed how I did the job. If I treated people with genuine respect, if I listened with something resembling empathy, I could reach them in ways that force never could. That stayed with me until the day I retired.

That is what the sociological imagination looks like from inside a badge. It does not make the job easier. It makes it honest.

Learning to Listen

A man reports a mugging. The screen shows a crime, a location, and a suspect description. A noise complaint at a commercial site looks like a nuisance call. The categories capture what happened and leave unexamined everything that produced it. A dispatcher who develops the sociological imagination goes beyond the category and into the conditions that generate the call, the neighborhood dealing with decades of disinvestment, the block where the same calls reappear in the log year after year because the conditions that produce them never get addressed.

A welfare check on an elderly woman living alone enters the queue flagged routine, a categorization that misses everything essential to understand the situation. She has not eaten in two days. A neighbor noticed the mail piling up. Decades of decisions moved elderly people out of extended family households, defunded home health programs, shuttered senior centers, and left neighbors too exhausted or too distant to notice until something goes wrong. She is one of thousands living inside the same abandonment, in the same city, on blocks that look different from each other and produce the same call. A dispatcher who sees beyond the call and into the conditions that produced it brings a different kind of attention to every person in the queue.

Every person builds their understanding of the world from the raw materials of their own experience within the immediate milieu of family, work, school, community, and interpersonal relationships. That knowledge is real, hard-won, and entirely our own. It is also, by its very nature, partial and myopic in ways we cannot see from inside it. None of us chose the small slice of human experience we were born into, and most of us never recognize the limitation because from inside our life, it feels like the whole world. It is not the whole world. It's a window onto the world, and every window has a frame.

The sociological imagination widens that frame. It does not invalidate what personal experience teaches us. It places that experience inside a vastly larger picture, one that includes the lives of people whose private worlds never touch ours, shaped by institutions and historical forces we never personally experience. For the dispatcher, that expansion goes beyond intellectual enrichment. It is the difference between hearing Derrick and truly *listening* to him, between recognizing anomie and filing it under difficult caller, between serving human rights and processing cases. It travels home.

Recognize Patterns Beyond Individual Behavior

It is 11:47 at night and a woman calls in a whisper. The dispatcher hears a television in the background, a door closing somewhere in the apartment, and then silence before she speaks again. She provides the address and stops. The dispatch screen pulls it up before she finishes. 15 calls this month. The dispatcher recognizes the address the way you recognize a face you have seen so many times under the wrong circumstances. She says she is fine now, that she does not need anyone dispatched, and she is sorry for calling. The dispatcher hears the specific cadence of someone who learned to shrink the emergency down to a size that will not make things worse. She is far from fine. She called 15 times this month, and she is still there, whispering, and apologizing for reaching out to the only number left to call.

Fifteen calls from the same address tell the dispatcher everything about the conditions keeping her there.

Economic dependence traps people in ways a call screen never shows. Leaving an abusive or threatening situation requires independent income, accessible housing, and available shelter beds. The absences that block those exits are rooted in conditions that long predate the call. Immigration status binds some people to abusive partners through fear of deportation or family separation. Childcare and employment form a closed loop with no clear exit. Legal protections exist on paper, but overburdened courts grind too slowly to help anyone experiencing immediate danger. Abusers sever their domestic partner's support networks deliberately, over months and years, until isolation becomes its own kind of captivity. Childhood exposure to violence reconstitutes what feels normal in ways that take years to recognize. When every bond of support disappears, some people turn to substances because the pain demands relief that nothing else provides.

A dispatcher who understands this hears the 15th call as confirmation that the conditions keeping her there persist. Knowing what drives the call makes it harder to treat the response as routine. If the dispatcher knows this, the officer walking through that door needs to know it too. What distinguishes a response that interrupts a cycle from one that simply documents it lives in the details. The dispatcher coordinates follow-up with social services, flags the call for a victim advocate, and frames the situation accurately for the officer heading to the door.

The same structural logic that traps a person inside a violent home operates on the block outside it. Randol Contreras documented how young men in economically marginalized neighborhoods turn to robbery, in this case robbing drug dealers, because legal paths to income closed off long before they were old enough to navigate economic exclusion (Contreras 2012). A dispatcher who receives the fourth call this week reporting theft from the same block holds four individual incidents, each with a suspect description and a case number. Those four calls together describe a neighborhood shaped by chronic unemployment, a grocery store that closed two years ago, a school that lost its vocational programs, and a visible economy offering little to a 19-year-old without a car or a credential. Knowing this does not excuse robbing people or dealing dope. But it situates the call within a larger reality, shifting the questions worth asking, the resources worth mentioning, and the picture passed along to the officer heading into that block for the fourth time this week.

What's Beyond Words

A woman calls saying she thinks an intruder is in the house. She lacks details, but her voice says everything. It trembles and strains to hold steady, the sound of someone holding herself together long enough to dial. Fear reaches the line before language. A dispatcher who recognizes fear in the voice knows what help needs to look like.

Listening requires a dispatcher to simultaneously track both what the caller reports and what the caller reveals. A caller reporting a sexual assault may go silent before answering a direct question. That silence reflects someone searching for words to describe what seems indescribable. People experiencing trauma rarely speak in clear sentences, especially under pressure. When a dispatcher waits through that silence without interrupting, allows the caller time to continue, and shows through tone and pacing that the caller's words are taken seriously, the caller feels heard and the responder arrives better prepared to help.

The pace of speech itself communicates something important. A parent reporting a missing child who repeats the same details, circles back, loses the thread, and starts over shows the dispatcher the depth of their fear. The repetition itself signals the alarm more accurately than its content. A dispatcher who responds to that urgency earns the trust the parent needs to slow down enough to provide the details required for a response.

A caller who describes a violent assault in a steady, distant tone, listing what happened as though recounting someone else's afternoon, speaks from a place where the mind has pulled back to survive telling the story. Nothing in the voice rises or breaks. A dispatcher hears calm and sends responders expecting composure. The door opens to someone unable to meet them eye to eye, who struggles to answer, whose body tells what the voice could not say.

Suspending Judgment

A domestic violence survivor calls for the first time after six months of escalating abuse. She waited because she feared retaliation and hoped something might somehow change. She feels shame with nowhere to place it, and to make the situation worse, her financial dependence makes leaving home feel like stepping off a ledge. She also fears for her children. Every word she chooses on this call reflects these pressures, including the decision to call at all. What she says, what she emphasizes, and what she leaves out reflect constraints the dispatcher cannot see from the console. How this call unfolds will influence whether she calls again when the next crisis arises or endures it alone and terrified, and whether the person she lives with finally receives an intervention already six months overdue.

Frequent callers reach out of desperation. They cycle through impossible situations because the conditions that drove them to call the first time persist long after the call ends. Every time they dial, they depend entirely on what they find on the other end of the line. A dispatcher who brings the same attention to the third call as to the first treats the repetition as relevant information. The calls continue because the situation accumulates. A dispatcher who understands this listens with fresh ears.

On her third call, her voice is flatter. She moves through the questions quickly, leaving out what was hard to say before. One dispatcher hears repetition and moves the call along. Another hears what's been building and waits one second longer, asks one more question, and gives her a different answer than the last two times.

Recognizing Context

A man calls to report a break-in at his home. His voice remains controlled, careful, and precise while he gives his address, describes what he heard, and answers every question. Then he adds that he is Black and wants the dispatcher to know he lives there. That single detail shows what history taught him about what can happen when officers assume who belongs inside a home. Understanding why he said it, and what it cost him to say it, changes how the dispatcher frames the call and what the responding officer encounters when help arrives.

People in neighborhoods with histories of over-policing, discrimination, and police violence call with a fear that developed across years and generations before the call happened (Bourgois 2003; Contreras 2012; Du Bois 1903). The dispatcher did not create that fear, but they stand at the exact moment where it gets either confirmed or contradicted. A dispatcher who recognizes where that caution originates responds with clarity and steadiness, framing the call in ways that prepare officers for the full human being they will meet rather than the version the screen produces on its own, a version without history, without the truth of who is behind that door.

A caller reaching the line for the first time arrives at the worst moment of their life into a process that feels routine to everyone but them. They may speak hesitantly, leave out details that seem obvious, or struggle to answer direct questions while fear overwhelms them. Some callers navigate this in a second language, searching for words that arrive slower but harder than the emergency demands. A dispatcher who slows down, speaks clearly, and reaches for translation services walks that caller through the worst moment of their day rather than moving them along like a case to be closed.

A dispatcher who understands why a man says he is Black and that he lives there sends officers to a home they enter with clearer eyes and gives that man a response that acknowledges what it took to say it.

Crisis Intervention Team Model: Verstehen in Practice

A family member calls to say her brother is behaving erratically. She sounds simultaneously frightened, exhausted, and embarrassed. What happens at the dispatch center in the next few minutes decides how this encounter proceeds. A dispatcher who frames it as a mental health emergency sends help in a guardian posture. This framing moves ahead of the response and influences what the brother will encounter when help arrives.

The Crisis Intervention Team model grew out of Memphis, Tennessee in the 1980s after a police shooting forced the department to confront what officers understood about mental illness. It places the person in crisis at the center of the response, connecting people to receive care rather than get arrested, and treats mental illness as a condition requiring treatment rather than a problem requiring control (Compton et al. 2008; Rogers, McNiel, and Binder 2019). All of this starts at the console, with how a dispatcher describes what they heard.

The sociological imagination allows the dispatcher to interpret the caller's experience within the historical forces and social conditions that shape it. Max Weber described this capacity as verstehen, the ability to understand another person's subjectivity while navigating tough circumstances (Weber 1922/1978). A sister calling about her brother has information the call log will never capture. She knows his baseline, what helped him in the past, and whether his behavior signals danger, confusion, or fear. A dispatcher who records only the present behavior strips away context and sends officers into a partial picture. A dispatcher who practices verstehen passes along that context to form a more complete picture so the response reflects the full situation.

The dispatcher's voice reaches the person in crisis before the officer. Speaking calmly to a frightened family member or the person in distress begins de-escalation while help is on the way. Asking what has previously worked, who the person trusts, and what they need signals that this call will show compassion to the person in distress. Those questions also yield information that changes the actions officers take at the scene.

Crisis lines, mobile mental health units, and co-responder teams work alongside or in place of police. The dispatcher hears the sister describing her brother and decides what kind of response arrives at the door. Will it be a patrol car sent alone, or officers briefed to slow down and wait for backup trained in de-escalation? The dispatcher makes this decision. The brother will never know what was said at the dispatch center, only what comes through the doorway.

Applying the Sociological Imagination

A woman calls, crying and frustrated. Her 14-year-old son missed 120 out of 180 school days this year. The school threatens legal action. She's got nowhere else to turn and no one left to call.

A child who misses two thirds of the school year signals that something makes attending school nearly impossible. Housing instability, unreliable transportation, bullying, undiagnosed learning disabilities, family responsibilities, chronic illness, and domestic violence rarely appear in the record of absences. A mother who calls 911 about truancy has tried the principal, the district office, and social services. As options dwindle, she faces legal action. The call itself becomes evidence that every other door closed and locked behind her.

A dispatcher who understands this opens with questions rather than redirection. What changed when the absences began? Can he get to school reliably? Is he safe at home? Has the school offered any support? These questions allow the real situation to emerge. The family lost their apartment six months ago when rent climbed beyond what two minimum-wage jobs afford. They sleep in their car or in shelters that bar children over 12 from the family section. They have no consistent address, reliable transportation, or quiet place for their son to do his homework. His clothes are dirty. Ashamed and exhausted, he stops trying. What looks like a truancy problem is a housing crisis unfolding where a family does everything right in a system where doing what's right is insufficient.

The dispatcher cannot rehouse this family, rewrite shelter policy, or compel the school district to do what it should have done months ago. What the dispatcher can do is understand this mother as someone the system failed rather than someone who failed the system. With this understanding, the dispatcher connects her to the appropriate resources. Social services can address immediate housing needs, school enrollment, and transportation. Under the 1987 McKinney-Vento Homeless Assistance Act, schools must enroll homeless students without proof of residency and provide transportation. Most families discover this only after the system failed them with its silence. The dispatcher explains it, provides the numbers she needs, and documents the call with full structural context intact, including homelessness, service needs, shelter policy separating her from her son, and the pattern of absences and their cause. That documentation moves the case forward in the family's favor. Everyone involved afterward works from an accurate picture rather than a truancy complaint that frames a desperate mother as a negligent one.

Storytelling and Human Rights

Humans are the makers of stories and the products of them (Smith 2003). The narratives we tell make and direct our lives, coloring our understanding of ourselves and of people whose private worlds we never encounter. But the stories told about the most vulnerable people are rarely their own. Long before a caller reaches the dispatch center, someone else already defined them. Stanley Cohen called them folk devils, people societies single out and scapegoat to blame for larger social problems, whose identities get transformed into threat, whose circumstances get reduced to individual pathology, and whose humanity gets defined by others (Cohen 1972/2011). What matters in these narratives is not the facts but rather, as Smith puts it, "the more significant story running through, over, and under 'the facts,' the story that itself constitutes what is a fact, what it is that matters" (Smith 2003, 66). Journalists, prosecutors, politicians, and academics theorize about communities they rarely encounter, and the narratives they produce travel through institutions the way rot moves through a structure, unseen and unquestioned, until the walls no longer hold.

Both caller and dispatcher have stories. Long before anyone dials emergency services, the media, politicians, and moral entrepreneurs have already written the story of the poor, immigrants, the mentally ill, the addicted, the racialized, and the criminalized. A dispatcher who grows up watching the news, scrolling headlines, internalizing years of messaging about who counts as dangerous and who deserves help – brings all of that to the dispatch center. The stories come first. The person they describe arrives second. The person almost never wins that race. These preconceptions determine who sounds credible, whose fear registers as real, and whose account gets recorded accurately. A dispatcher who never examines these stories acts on them anyway, and the caller on the other end of the line pays the price.

A woman calls to report that her neighbor assaulted her. The dispatcher gathers the address and a description, what the call requires. The woman keeps talking. She describes weeks of harassment, a landlord ignoring her complaints, and the patterns of abuse she tried to document alone. The dispatch system has what it needs. That is the moment when the dispatcher decides whether to stay with what the caller is still trying to say.

Every caller deserves the chance to represent themselves. Letting someone finish reflects the opposite of what institutions have done for years to people with the least power. Marginalized people lose the right to speak for themselves so consistently that they feel the loss before they dial. A dispatcher who interrupts, assumes, or stops listening before the caller finishes decides whose account is taken as authoritative and whose is managed as a problem.

Professional judgment still governs the call. A dispatcher cannot hold every line indefinitely. But a dispatcher can distinguish between ending a call after gathering enough information to guide the response and ending it while the caller is still describing what happened. One decision truncates the account and leaves holes in what gets recorded. The other completes the exchange once the dispatcher can act and lets the caller finish their account.

When a caller says someone grabbed her throat, preventing her from breathing, those words belong in the record exactly as said. Reducing her account to domestic assault preserves the category and erases the person. The caller remains the person who knows best what happened to her even when her story appears fragmented, contradictory, and emotionally raw. A dispatcher who preserves her words rather than translating them into institutional shorthand gives officers, advocates, and prosecutors an account that reflects what happened rather than what the dispatch system found convenient to record. Telling her that what she described sounds frightening, that she did the right thing by calling, costs nothing. For the caller, it can mean everything.

Double Consciousness When Calling 911

Two uneven identities, one person. I never fully reconciled these two conflicting identities. I grew up American but never quite fit. My parents brought Cuba with them when they arrived to Miami and gave me a sense of Cubanidad that remains. I even sought it out, traveling to Cuba as a teenager against my parents' wishes to connect with the land of my people. Cuba lived in our household in the food, the music, the Spanish that filled every room, and in the way my family understood loyalty, struggle, triumph, and endurance. I absorbed all of it. I also absorbed the United States with its urban schools, city streets, cultural expectations, and unwavering insistence that you assimilate or remain outside. I lived in both worlds but never fully belonged to either.

That sense of being split in two sharpened when I moved to Wisconsin and joined the faculty of a predominantly white university. I was present in every room and absent at the same time. I sat at tables where I was the only person who looked and acted like me or understood what it meant to live inside two worlds that never fully reconciled. I earned my place, yet the dean and chair subjected me to what they called "impression management mentoring," nothing more than behavior modification training meant to change my behavior and remake me in their image, a systematic attempt to eliminate who I am and replace it with who they wanted me to become. They launched it. I stopped them, but not before they made clear what institutions do to people who refuse to be remade. Societies that modify the behavior of individuals who refuse to conform to the dominant image have a name in the historical record.

W.E.B. Du Bois's brilliant book *The Souls of Black Folk* described the double consciousness as the experience of living in a society that refuses to see you fully while you constantly measure yourself through the eyes of a world that offers contempt rather than full recognition of your humanity (Du Bois 1903). That two-ness means having both your own sense of self and the version others impose on you. Those prewritten narratives tell callers what to expect before anyone answers the phone. A dispatcher who has never felt that two-ness can still learn to recognize it in the voice on the line. A dispatcher who has felt it already understands the cost of reaching for help while anticipating how the system will see you.

A Black man calls to report a break-in. He gives the location and tells the dispatcher he is Black. He wants her to know he lives there. That single detail holds the gravity of everything history taught him. It reflects what he already knows about how quickly presence becomes suspicion when officers hit the scene without the proper context. In the span of one call, he manages two emergencies at once, the break-in and the pending encounter with police. Managing this takes effort. It requires monitoring his voice, choosing words that signal calm rather than fear, and presenting himself as a resident before anyone questions his place in the home. A dispatcher who understands that effort does more than collect facts. They treat the call as a life rather than a report and frame the response so officers arrive prepared for the full person at the door, not some flattened, stereotyped version of him.

An immigrant woman calls about domestic violence. She faces immediate danger as well as the awareness that every word she speaks travels through law enforcement systems that decide whether she belongs in the country she now calls home, whether asking for help could bring immigration scrutiny, and whether safety reaches her or creates new risk. She pauses before dialing, listens to the sound of the house around her, and makes the call anyway while keeping her voice steady enough to avoid drawing the wrong kind of attention.

A dispatcher working strictly with standard procedure collects an address, an incident type, and a description of assault, then moves to the next call. A dispatcher who listens to what that moment costs her hears something else entirely, a woman speaking carefully because she knows that panic, accent, or the wrong word can change what happens next, a person reaching for help while also calculating the cost of asking for it.

The First 30 Seconds

A woman calls distraught about her teenage son who hasn't made it home. The terror in her voice reaches the dispatchers ears before the words. She struggles to find the right English under pressure, repeating herself, losing the thought, and starting over. A dispatcher who treats that struggle as a reason to disengage tells her to calm down, explains that he cannot understand her, informs her of a 24-hour waiting period, and closes the call. In under a minute, her fear goes unrecognized while the dispatch system records the interaction as handled. Her son is still missing.

A dispatcher who slows down, speaks clearly, and asks simple questions opens a different world for the person on the other end. Immigrant families reaching emergency services bring a history of what happens when people like them ask for help. They learned, through experience and watching what happens to others like them, that calling for help can cost more than remaining silent. This mother knew this before she dialed, and called anyway. The dispatcher lets her speak in her own words, accesses translation services, and documents her account as she gives it rather than flattening it into institutional shorthand. When she hesitates, the dispatcher tells her she did the right thing by calling and that the goal is to find her son.

What emerges from the conversation reveals that the son is 15, he left for school that morning and never got there, his absence is entirely unlike him, and the immigrant family is still navigating a new country, a new language, and a new life. The dispatcher documents everything with the full context intact, connects the mother to resources, and passes the situation to responding officers with the framing it requires. A 15-year-old who left for school and never arrived, a mother describing behavior completely out of character, a family that needs support along with a search for the son.

Derrick called about the heat. This mother called about her son. The calls look nothing alike. They are the same call, a person at the end of their options reaching for the one line left. This mother needed someone to hear that her child was missing, that she was terrified, and that she had been failed before but was calling anyway. Everything this chapter argues for depends on the decision a dispatcher makes in the first 30 seconds, before the queue builds, before momentum pushes forward and the moment closes.

References

Bourgois, Philippe. 2003. *In Search of Respect: Selling Crack in El Barrio*. 2nd ed. Cambridge: Cambridge University Press.

Cohen, Stanley. 2011. *Folk Devils and Moral Panics: The Creation of the Mods and Rockers*. Routledge Classics ed. Abingdon: Routledge. Originally published 1972.

Compton, Michael T., Manya Bahora, Amy C. Watson, and Janet R. Oliva. 2008. "A Comprehensive Review of Extant Research on Crisis Intervention Team (CIT) Programs." *Journal of the American Academy of Psychiatry and the Law* 36 (1): 47–55.

Contreras, Randol. 2012. *The Stickup Kids: Race, Drugs, Violence, and the American Dream*. Berkeley: University of California Press.

Du Bois, W. E. B. 1903. *The Souls of Black Folk*. Chicago: A. C. McClurg & Co.

Durkheim, Émile. 1897. *Suicide: A Study in Sociology*. Translated by John A. Spaulding and George Simpson. New York: Free Press, 1951.

Mills, C. Wright. 1959. *The Sociological Imagination*. New York: Oxford University Press.

Rogers, Michael S., Dale E. McNiel, and Renée L. Binder. 2019. "Effectiveness of Police Crisis Intervention Training Programs." *Journal of the American Academy of Psychiatry and the Law* 47 (4). https://doi.org/10.29158/JAAPL.003863-19.

Smith, Christian. 2003. *Moral, Believing Animals: Human Personhood and Culture*. New York: Oxford University Press.

Weber, Max. 1978. *Economy and Society: An Outline of Interpretive Sociology*. Edited by Guenther Roth and Claus Wittich. Berkeley: University of California Press. Originally published 1922.

Chapter 4

Three People, One Call

An Ordinary Sunday Morning Backlog

Lieutenant Pedro Marina describes one of his calls as Platoon Commander of the Third District, New Orleans Police Department.

> Police work is more than just law enforcement. It is a public service that no other agency can provide, if for no other reason than the fact that it operates 24 hours a day, seven days a week. I performed this job for nearly 30 years in many capacities, from years in the narcotics enforcement unit to patrol officer as well as unit supervisor and commander. In keeping with that vital component of public service, especially as a district platoon supervisor, I often considered input from the police dispatcher in prioritizing and assigning calls for service. I am thinking of that time when I was working in the Third District as a platoon commander and I got to work on a Sunday morning at 7 a.m. to discover a backlog of some 20 calls left by the night platoon. In looking at my computer to monitor the flow of calls being assigned to my platoon officers as they left roll call, I noticed that the dispatcher was using not only the time that the call came in, but also the gravity of the situations by those citizens looking for police help. There was a call about an accident on the interstate that had been waiting for three hours. She dispatched that immediately. There was another call about a drunk in a bar causing trouble, about five hours old. I was just noticing the call on my screen when she called to tell me that she had called the complainant at the bar to learn that the drunk was long gone and the bar was closing. The dispatcher wanted to know if she could mark up the call as unfounded just to get rid of it. Of course, I replied that she could assign it to me and mark it up. A few minutes later the dispatcher called me again, this time by phone, to tell me that there was a call in the backlog from a woman who stated that her sick and obese husband had fallen out of bed and she could not lift him. The call was about two

DOI: 10.4324/9781003583868-4

hours old. Imagining what these people were going through, I instructed the dispatcher to call the complainant to find out if the problem had been solved. She called and said the man was okay but still on the floor and the wife was crying. I looked at my screen and noted that the backlog was coming down but still included two burglaries, an auto theft, and a robbery that would normally only be handled by a police officer, not a supervisor or commander. However, I could help the sick man on the floor. I just needed a sergeant to meet me there and help me lift this man without hurting him. I advised the dispatcher to assign the call to me and have one of the two platoon sergeants meet me at the location. I knew there was some heavy lifting involved in this call for service. I arrived at the location, met the sergeant, and the two of us lifted the man back to his bed. In the middle of that, the dispatcher called me saying that she had located an EMS unit available if we needed one. I replied that there was no need, the man was fine, and everybody was happy. A bit later in the morning, dispatch called me on the phone asking how heavy the man was. I replied jokingly that he was not too heavy for the strong arm of the law. We both laughed.

Tri-Subject Asymmetry

The morning backlog that Lieutenant Pedro Marina walked into held people fixed at different points along the same chain of decisions. A woman remained in her home beside her husband, who had been on the floor for two hours, unable to get up or call for help. The officers leaving roll call faced a queue of burglaries, a stolen car, and a robbery awaiting assignment. They would go where they were sent, arriving with only the information dispatch provided.

At the center of the situation sat the dispatcher. She returned to the call, picked up the phone again, and confirmed that nothing had changed. The man was still on the floor. The wife was still waiting. She kept the call active, maintained its priority, and updated responding officers as new information became available. The lieutenant decided to take the call while requesting a sergeant to meet him at the location. When they arrived, the dispatcher remained connected to the call and arranged additional assistance without being prompted.

Three people participated in that call without meeting. One asked for help. One needed it. One responded after taking the call, acting on the information provided by dispatch. The flow of information through the dispatcher linked all three participants, each update influencing what happened next and how long the man remained on the floor. The dispatcher did not control the outcome but mediated what each participant could know and when they could act. This produced a structured asymmetry in which the caller, the subject of the call, and the responding officer occupied the same event without sharing the same knowledge, access, or capacity to intervene at the same moment.

The dispatcher does not stand between two people. The dispatcher stands at the center of three: the caller who speaks, the person the call concerns who never does, and the officer moving toward a scene the dispatcher built from words before a single wheel turned. Each possesses full human rights that the dispatcher is obligated to protect, yet each enters the dispatcher's decisions from a position of asymmetry, with unequal voice, unequal access, and unequal ability to influence what the dispatch center produces. This is the tri-subject asymmetry: the dispatcher's simultaneous obligation to protect the human rights of the caller, the person the call concerns, and the responding officer. The officer is not merely an instrument of dispatch. She arrives carrying her own rights, her own safety, and her own exposure to the consequences of what the dispatcher chose to send into a scene.

The same three obligations arrive differently when the call involves a racial description, no confirmed threat, and a framing decision that will reach a man who never made the call and has no voice in how he is described.

It is 2:40 pm when the call comes in. A woman reports a man behaving erratically outside a convenience store on the corner of Broad and Dumaine. Her voice is steady, careful. She wants the situation handled without escalation. She says he is pacing, talking to himself, moving in ways that frightened her when she walked past. But she does not say he threatened her or that he has a weapon. She also says he is a large Black man and wants someone to check on him.

The dispatcher now faces a decision on how to frame the call. She can dispatch it as "erratic subject, possible threat," calling officers to pull up expecting a confrontation. She can also dispatch "man in distress, welfare check requested" where officers will arrive with room to assess what they find. She can further note that no threat was made, no weapon reported, and that the description reflects a caller's fear rather than an observed danger. Or she can dispatch the call forward without that distinction, letting the caller's alarm become fact before officers make the scene.

The officer hears the call before opening the car door. What comes over the radio determines how the officer positions herself, how her hands move, and how she makes contact. It also frames what she expects to find before she sees a single face. The man outside the store remains unaware that a call was made. He has no voice in how he is described or what information is sent to the officer. He will meet the response the dispatcher set in motion.

Core Principles: The Foundation

Human rights dispatching follows four principles that govern every call and decision a dispatcher makes under pressure. Together they ground the dispatcher's simultaneous obligation to three human beings.

Principle 1: Human Rights Belong to Everyone the Call Reaches

Every person who calls 911 possesses full human rights, regardless of criminal history, tone of voice, frequency of prior contact, mental state, sobriety, housing status, documentation, hostility, confusion, race, ethnicity, religion, national origin, age, disability, health condition, occupation, or involvement in criminalized economies. Each represents a characteristic that dispatchers and institutions have used to decide that some callers deserve less attention and compassion. Yet every caller comes on the line in full possession of rights that remain intact regardless of what any characteristic says about them.

Durkheim's concept of anomie explains the subjective feelings of uncertainty and meaninglessness that happen when the social world breaks down. Applied to the dispatcher's console, anomie reveals why so many people call emergency services broken, exhausted, and beyond their limit (Durkheim 1897/1951). When the institutions that organize social life collapse, fracture, or systematically exclude people from access to power, wealth, and resources necessary to build a coherent life, the individuals within those institutions experience anomie, the profound disorientation of a life stripped of meaning, direction, and social connection. Anomie is not a metaphor for hardship. When hurricanes devastate a city and the infrastructure of daily life disappears overnight, when bombs drop on neighborhoods and the institutions that once organized existence cease to function, when economies collapse and work vanishes and the social fabric tears faster than anyone can repair it, suicide rates climb among ordinary people and among the officers and first responders whose sense of purpose depended on the very order that collapsed around them. The protectors become the unprotected, and anomie claims them too.

Anomie does not necessarily require catastrophe to do its damage. It can build slowly through social exclusion, denied access to the institutions, and the grinding experience of watching a society's promises unravel. The homeless caller, the person in mental health crisis, and the frequent caller with nowhere else to turn did not choose those conditions. Broken institutions and structural contradictions produce them.

If we live in a sick and broken society, then how can the person well-adjusted to it claim mental health? If a society produces isolation, instability, and conditions that strip people of connection, security, and meaning, then adjustment to that society cannot be the measure of mental health. As individuals, we are forced to become socialized into a sick social world. When that socialization works, and we become well-adjusted to that sick society, we in turn become sick and mentally ill, even when that sickness wears the face of normalcy and happiness. Erich Fromm argues that mental health cannot be defined by how well individuals adapt to social demands, but by whether a society meets follow human needs and supports human development (Fromm 1955). In a disordered society, what passes as normal often reflects a shared psychological strain, a pattern of adaptation that buries harm beneath the appearance of functioning. Fromm describes the cost of remaining fully human under these conditions. A person who continues to feel, who refuses to become numb, who does not turn themselves into an object to survive, often experiences doubt, isolation, and distress not because they are unwell, but because they see clearly the conditions others have learned to accept as normal. Their suffering reflects the strain of clarity in a world that rewards disconnection. Or, as Krishnamurti is often quoted as saying, "It is no measure of health to be well adjusted to a profoundly sick society."

The caller is only one of three rights-bearing subjects the dispatcher is obligated to protect. The person the call concerns has those same rights in an encounter the dispatcher's words construct, the right to be presumed innocent, the right to dignity, the right to life and security, and the right to a response proportionate to what is happening. The officer holds rights too. The rights of responding officers must be protected the moment dispatch sends the call. An officer who is told to expect a threat steps out of the car with a different posture, grip, and threshold for force than an officer told to expect uncertainty. If that expectation rests on assumption rather than what the caller reported, the dispatcher places that officer in a position where hesitation becomes dangerous and escalation becomes necessary. A dispatcher who protects one person while abandoning another fails to practice human rights dispatching.

Principle 2: Dispatchers Shape the Experience of Rights

Dispatchers make the difference between callers possessing rights and experiencing them in the first seconds of a call. Callers recognize immediately if a dispatcher responds to their situation with full attention or with tempered impatience. They can tell whether they are being asked to explain what is happening or to defend themselves, whether their account is validated or treated with skepticism.

A woman who reports a break-in gets cut off with questions about the certainty of her claim. A man who reports a threat is questioned if anything happened at all. A teenager who calls reporting a violent event is told to slow down, start over, and speak clearly. In each case, the opening exchange shows whether the caller will be believed, questioned, or dismissed.

The first question sets that direction in motion. "What is your emergency?" opens a story. "Are you sure someone broke in?" turns alarm into doubt before the details emerge. "Start from the beginning" can steady a shaking voice or force someone already overwhelmed to relive a traumatic event. The dispatcher can now either allow a caller to describe what they saw, heard, and feared, or narrow them to answers that fit preset categories. One path holds the situation together. The other reduces it until only a label remains.

Nothing about this appears consequential from an outsider's perspective, but within the call it is constant interpretation under pressure. Each exchange either clarifies what is happening or replaces it with something easier to process on a screen. The version of the situation the dispatcher chooses to send moves ahead of the officer, informing how they prepare for the encounter, how they read the first movements they see, and how quickly they decide what kind of situation they now face. Recall the call at Broad and Dumaine, where the dispatcher faced exactly this decision. She could send to responding officers what the caller feared, or she could send what the caller reported. That framing decision would arrive with the officer before a single door opened, and it would meet a man who had no voice in how he was described. A dispatcher who sends the wrong version does not just misdescribe a scene. She puts an officer on the ground expecting danger that does not exist, and she puts a man outside a store in the path of a response he did nothing to deserve. Both may not walk away from that decision.

Principle 3: Restrict Rights Only When Necessary and Proportionate

Real threats exist, and some calls require dispatchers to limit privacy, autonomy, or discretion to prevent harm. A person holding a weapon inside a home may require immediate police response. A caller expressing intent to end his life may demand emergency intervention without delay. A report that begins as confidential may need to be shared when another person's life is at risk. These moments test the framework of human rights.

Proportionate action begins with what the dispatcher hears and verifies in the call itself. A dispatcher listens to the caller's words, tracks events as they unfold, and asks questions that pin down what is happening. Instead of turning ambiguity into conclusion, the dispatcher constructs the account as it happens, records what the caller reports, what sounds come through the background, how the voice changes under pressure, and what specific actions or threats the caller describes. That discipline allows officers to arrive at the scene with an account they can act on with confidence.

A mental health crisis labeled "combative" or "noncompliant" pulls force into a room where fear, confusion, or acute distress drives behavior. The system meets the person in crisis as a threat. Every decision that follows locks in that framing, escalates response, and increases the risk of harm for everyone involved.

The same framing moves ahead of the responder, settling into their expectations prior to making the scene. An officer expecting resistance operates differently than one expecting uncertainty and distress. Their expectations change their distance, tone, and the speed at which force becomes an option, affecting both the officer's safety and the safety of the person they encounter. One officer prepares for confrontation even when none is present. The other officer has room to recognize a frightened human being before deciding how to respond. The dispatcher's words set the conditions for the first contact on the scene.

Proportionate restriction responds to what happens in the call, grounded in what the caller reports and what the dispatcher verifies, determining whether intervention protects life or increases risk. In human rights dispatching, safety and dignity depend on the same accuracy. When separated, restriction stops functioning as protection and begins producing the very harm it was meant to prevent.

The call at Broad and Dumaine required exactly that discipline. No threat was reported. No weapon was described. Dispatching "erratic subject, possible threat" would not have responded to what happened on that call. It would have responded to what the dispatcher allowed the caller's fear to become.

Principle 4: Professional Agency Extends Beyond Routine

Protocol provides structure and consistency when calls come in faster than anyone can think and the queue never fully clears. It ensures calls move, captures information, and coordinates responses under pressure. But protocol cannot account for every form of human vulnerability within each call. Each shift presents moments that must go beyond procedure alone.

Dispatchers exercise professional agency in how they process those moments. They slow the pace of a call when panic overtakes the caller's words instead of rushing the call toward completion. They distinguish between a situation that signals deliberate harm and one that shows fear, confusion, or crisis before assigning a response that avoids treating them as the same. They move forward details that would otherwise be lost, preserving what the caller said. They pass along context so responders understand the situation at hand. They stay on the line during moments of silence because the caller is still trying to form what happened into words. None of these actions appear in a checklist, but each one determines how the dispatcher codes and describes the call. Each decision changes what the caller hears, what the officer expects, and what the person on the scene will face.

These decisions accumulate under pressure, often without recognition and often under constraint. Within that constraint, dispatchers decide how much of a situation to build before sending officers out, what to record from the caller's words, what to pull from background sound, and what to ask to clarify the ongoing situation. Such choices determine whether the response protects people or performs bureaucratic efficiency, stripping away important details. Dispatchers stay with hesitation in a caller's voice, catch changes in breathing, note repeated details, and track what does not fit. That kind of attention disciplines judgment during each call. The dispatcher from Lieutenant Marina's story called back a crying wife, kept the man on the floor alive in her queue, and picked up the phone again when nothing had changed. She was practicing human rights dispatching, holding the caller, the man on the floor, and the officers she would send all inside the same sustained attention.

The Seven Rights Most Relevant to Dispatching

The Universal Declaration of Human Rights and the International Covenant on Civil and Political Rights emerged from the 20th century's most catastrophic failures of institutional power. The Holocaust revealed with terrible clarity what happens when state bureaucracies turn the law, police authority, and administrative systems into instruments of mass detention and extermination, targeting six million Jews along with Roma and Sinti, disabled people, political dissidents, Soviet prisoners of war, and others through a machinery of racial law, forced labor, and state violence. These human rights documents also reflect wartime internment, the targeting of noncombatant populations, and the collapse of legal protections under governments that converted administrative authority into instruments of harm. Seven of these rights surface repeatedly in emergency communication, and each one lands differently at the console than it does on the page.

The Right to Life and Security of Person

This right serves as the foundation of every other right in the framework because, without it, nothing else the caller needs can be realized. A person dialing 911 asserts, explicitly or not, that their safety takes precedence over efficiency, credibility assessments, or concerns about resource strain. When someone reports a threat to life, or believes they face one, that call requires an immediate response.

Violations of the right to life and security of person surface in response times that stretch unevenly across neighborhoods, when a dispatcher delays classification while a caller continues describing a threat, when immediate dispatch shifts into additional questioning because the voice does not match what the dispatcher expects, and when early judgments form while the caller is still speaking, turning what is unfolding into "unverified," "possible dispute," or "low priority" instead of dispatching it as a threat to life. A woman calls from a neighborhood that has long been treated as lower priority in emergency response, her voice controlled but strained, describing danger unfolding as it happens. The dispatcher who recognizes the address before fully hearing the account begins filtering her words through expectation instead of attending to them as they are spoken, and what she hears is no longer what she said, but what the dispatcher expected to hear.

This right extends to the responder as well. When context drops out, qualifiers disappear, and urgency flattens, the dispatcher builds a version of events that first appears on the screen and then directs movement in the field, sending it toward a human. What arrives at the scene is not only what happened, but also what the dispatcher sent as happening. A routine call triggers a potential threat. A confused situation escalates into a resistance scenario. A moment of fear gets coded as a category of danger. The right to life moves in both directions at once. The dispatcher's framing does not stop at the caller. It moves ahead of the officer and determines what the subject of the call will face.

The Right to Dignity

Human rights go far beyond dignity. Dignity marks a baseline, a necessary but insufficient condition for the realization of human rights. A dispatcher can speak in a calm, professional tone and still participate in a response that strips a person of their human rights. Courtesy alone does not preserve dignity.

A woman calls after being shoved in a shared apartment hallway. She stands outside her door, one hand pressed against her ribs, speaking carefully, so her voice does not break. The dispatcher hears her pause between sentences and the way she checks every word before she says it. The dispatcher notes the address, confirms the nature of the incident, and clears the required fields. The screen fills with categories, "domestic disturbance," "possible dispute," "verbal escalation." Nothing in those terms reflects the woman standing in the hallway trying to keep her breathing steady while she decides whether to stay or go.

A caller who sounds guarded or defensive has often spent years learning what happens when landlords, officers, or agencies treat hesitation as deception and fear as inconsistency. The dispatcher who reads that guardedness as obstruction turns the call into suspicion and the woman into a problem to be managed. The dispatcher who recognizes that guardedness as a response to past institutional failure leaves the woman seen. The dispatcher who codes the call and moves on leaves her reduced to a domestic disturbance code that will never reflect what happened to her body in that hallway, what she was protecting when she chose every word carefully, or what it cost her to make the call at all. Of the three subjects the dispatcher holds simultaneously, the caller is most exposed here. Dignity is determined in the first exchange, before the dispatcher knows anything about what happened, before any officer moves, and before the person the call concerns entered the picture at all.

The Right to Equal Protection Without Discrimination

Bias rarely surfaces in a form a dispatcher can name during the call. It surfaces in how calls are treated differently. Some accounts proceed without interruption. Others stop for additional questioning before a single unit moves. Some locations trigger immediate dispatch the moment the address enters the system. Others trigger doubt before the caller finishes speaking. These differences accumulate inside routine workflow, invisible to anyone reviewing the log afterward, because nothing in the record shows what did not happen or how long it took to happen. A man calls from a neighborhood that the 911 dispatch center repeatedly associates with frequent incidents. He stands inside his apartment describing a break currently unfolding in another room, his voice tight with effort as he tracks what he is hearing on the other side of the door. The dispatcher begins entering additional questions about certainty and detail while the call remains open on the screen, asking him to confirm what he saw and how he knows what he is describing. Across the city, similar reports are dispatched without that friction.

A woman calls from a shelter to report an assault outside the building. She speaks quickly, tries to compress what happened before losing her place. The dispatcher pauses on the coding screen, selects "incident unclear," and routes it beneath higher-priority calls describing property theft and traffic disruption from more affluent areas. Nothing in the moment makes the change visible. The difference is a field selection, a classification choice, a moment of interpretation that determines when prepared officers will be when they hit the scene.

A homeless man reports an attack near a transit station. He gives details, then hesitates, searching for words as wind cuts through the line and cold drains his focus. The dispatcher asks him to repeat himself twice, clarifying location and sequence, then assigns a code that will not trigger an immediate response. His account breaks into fragments shaped by exposure and exhaustion, and the system reduces it to what fits its categories.

In each of these cases, a different caller enters the same system of interpretation, where urgency is either accelerated or delayed through routine classification.

Callers hear the difference in the silence after they speak, in the speed of the questions that follow, in whether their urgency produces action or doubt. The officer rarely bears the cost of this failure. The caller and the person the call concerns do, in response time, resource allocation, and the kind of help that arrives.

The Right to Privacy

When callers describe a medical condition, a psychiatric history, or the details of a violent relationship, they speak while a dispatcher enters what they say into fields of type, priority, location, and a written account that will be read again later. A woman reports a recent psychiatric hospitalization while trying to keep her voice steady. A man names a medication he takes to manage panic that escalates under stress. A caller mentions a protective order issued months earlier and waits while the dispatcher confirms what the caller said. Each detail enters the record, stored in screens, reports, and dispatch notes that other eyes will later read.

Callers already know what happens when personal information leaves the moment it is spoken. A diagnosis mentioned during a prior response later appears in a court document. A history of treatment appears in a report read by officers who make the scene without having heard the person describe it themselves. A single sentence spoken in haste becomes part of a record that outlives the emergency that produced it. That knowledge influences what callers say and what they hold back while they are still on the line.

Protecting privacy means entering only what the response requires. A dispatcher records the information, confirms it, and enters it into the official narrative of the event knowing other eyes will read it later. What is withheld stays with the caller. The subject of the call and the officer do not surrender private information to dispatch. The caller does, and they do it during an ongoing emergency.

The Right to Be Presumed Innocent

A dispatcher receives a burglary call at 2:13 a.m. A neighbor reports seeing a man standing near the side entrance of an apartment building, hands in his pockets, looking toward parked cars. The caller says he "seems suspicious." The dispatcher types the description into the incident log. In one version of the entry, the man becomes "male standing near side entrance." In another, the word "suspicious" remains attached to him when the call transmits to responding officers. That single word travels ahead of the person it describes and settles into the officer's expectations before contact.

A second call comes in from a resident who reports movement behind a house. The caller describes someone walking along a fence line, pausing near a back door, then continuing down the alley. The dispatcher asks what the person did, what direction they moved, and what could be seen from the caller's window. The difference between those answers determines whether the dispatcher records observed movement or labels a person "lurking" behind a residence. Officers read that language before they see the person it describes.

Every call produces a written account that outlives the call that produced it. A dispatcher decides whether that account contains only what was reported or if it includes fear, assumption, or interpretation. Once entered, those words follow the person they describe, appearing on screens in patrol cars and handheld devices before physical contact. The person at the center of the report never sees those lines, but those lines guide the officer's first actions and expectations at the door before seeing a face or hearing a voice. Of the three subjects, the person the call concerns bears this right most fully and most vulnerably, because they never speak, never clarify, and never see the words the dispatcher chose to describe them.

Freedom From Torture and Cruel, Degrading Treatment

A dispatcher answers a call from a property manager reporting a tenant in a second-floor unit shouting through walls, pacing the apartment, and refusing to open the door. The dispatcher enters the details as the caller describes them, then asks what the tenant is shouting, what is being thrown, and whether anyone tried to enter the apartment. Each response the dispatcher records influences what officers expect when they pull up. The dispatcher can frame the situation as a person yelling inside an apartment and refusing to open the front door, or escalate it into a violent psychiatric emergency.

In a second call of similar type, a neighbor reports hearing a man inside an apartment crying out that he cannot breathe after several days without sleep. The dispatcher records prior mental health history that appears in the system, notes recent housing instability, and documents that no weapons have been seen or mentioned. That information enters the record alongside the real-time description and is read by every officer before arrival. One version emphasizes threat indicators such as "out of control" or "combative." Another version centers on observable behavior and known context without escalation language.

Both versions leave the console the same way, but they produce different expectations at the door. Officers entering the situation with a narrative of danger prepare for immediate control and rapid containment. Officers who arrive expecting distress and vulnerability have room to talk before force becomes the answer. The difference begins in the dispatcher's choices about what to enter, what to repeat back, and what to bring into the record that decides the nature of the encounter. The dispatcher's language determines what happens to both the subject and the officer. One faces the response the dispatcher built from words spoken by someone who was not in the room. The other arrives prepared for a threat that may exist only in the record. When that record is wrong, the person inside the apartment pays for it.

The Right to Effective Remedy

For many callers, 911 becomes the last working channel after every other institution seems closed. A parent calls the landlord about a threat in the building and receives no response. A student's caregiver contacts the school multiple times about harassment only to watch each report disappear into voicemail. A patient leaves messages with a clinic only to wait weeks without follow-up. By the time they reach dispatch, they are no longer starting a process. They are ending one.

A dispatcher opens the call log, enters the address, and types a brief account as the caller speaks. The dispatcher asks whether police have already been contacted, whether school staff or a landlord have been notified, whether a clinic or crisis line has been called, and what each of those contacts accomplished, if anything. Each answer gets written into the narrative box that follows the call to responding units. Those answers determine whether the call is dispatched as a narrow request for a unit or as a situation requiring coordination beyond police response, including social services, medical evaluation, or school intervention. The dispatcher writes the narrative that responders will read, deciding whether they show up prepared to address a single incident or a pattern that has broken every prior point of contact.

The truancy call in Chapter 3 illustrates this. A caregiver reports repeated school absences tied to escalating instability at home. The dispatcher documents not only the absence but also the failed attempts to resolve it through the school system, then transmits a description that frames the response around underlying need. An effective remedy occurs when the dispatcher refuses to reduce a broken chain of failed institutions to a single incident and instead transmits the full truth of what the caller has already survived trying to get help. The subject of the call and the officer enter the situation the dispatcher transmits. The caller is the only one who arrived already knowing the remedy had failed everywhere else.

Dispatch Language and Use of Force

Officers hear the language dispatchers use through radio transmissions and in-car screens before they observe a single fact on scene. Officers act on that information before their own eyes confirm anything.

Research on police use of force supports this relationship. Terrill and Mastrofski (2002) show that officers escalate force when they perceive higher levels of threat. The dispatcher contributes to that perception through the language entered in the call narrative and sent to responding units. When a dispatcher enters terms such as "violent," "escalating," or "dangerous subject," those labels appear in dispatch notes, read out over the radio during dispatch, and remain visible on screens while officers are en route.

That early framing changes how officers approach the location. They position themselves at a greater distance, keep hands near their weapons, and scan for rapid or unpredictable movement as they close in. They interpret hesitation, confusion, or sudden motion through a lens formed from the information they received before arrival. Stoughton (2014) documents how this anticipatory orientation narrows officer attention toward control and command presence while the scene still exists only in language.

That narrowing changes what officers allow themselves to see. Ambiguous behavior gets sorted more quickly into categories of threat. Time for assessment contracts. When dispatch language inflates or amplifies danger, officers enter encounters structured by a narrative formed before any observation. When dispatch language remains grounded in observable behavior and verified details, officers enter the scene with more interpretive room to assess what is happening. The physical scene does not change, but what the dispatcher sends off influences how officers anticipate, justify, and sometimes apply force.

Charles Kinsey, Narrative Framing, and Dispatcher Power

In July 2016 in North Miami, Florida, behavioral therapist Charles Kinsey lay on the ground with his hands raised beside an autistic patient holding a toy truck (BBC News 2016). Officers surrounded them with weapons drawn after responding to a 911 call reporting a man who might have a gun. Kinsey had no weapon. The patient held no weapon. One officer shot Kinsey in the leg anyway.

The 911 caller described a situation of uncertainty. She reported what she thought she saw and stated that she could not confirm whether a weapon was present. That uncertainty entered the call record, attached to a location and a request for response, and traveled toward officers already en route. The qualification did not survive transmission in its original form.

By the time officers arrived, they encountered a scene already organized around a potential threat. Kinsey lay on the ground with his hands raised and told officers repeatedly that he was unarmed and that the object nearby was a toy truck. Officers did not treat those statements as the primary framework for interpretation. They read the scene through the expectation of danger the dispatch record had already installed in their minds.

North Miami's police chief later confirmed that officers approached the scene expecting a possible armed subject (BBC News 2016). That expectation determined how officers interpreted the movement, language, and posture of the patient and his caretaker. Kinsey's raised hands and verbal reassurance did not reset the frame already formed prior to entering the scene.

Dispatchers control what enters the call record, how uncertainty is documented, and what language gets forwarded to responding units. Those choices color what officers perceive before a single firsthand observation.

The consequences of that framing extend to everyone involved. Kinsey faced officers who interpreted the encounter through a pre-established threat narrative. The officer who fired acted within a perception the dispatcher's words constructed, never tested against what the eyes saw.

Human rights dispatching resists converting uncertainty into certainty. It preserves qualifying language such as "possibly," "unclear," or "unconfirmed" rather than hardening it into a threat. That discipline keeps open the difference between what is known and assumed. In cases like Kinsey's, that difference determines whether officers show up to manage a confirmed danger or to assess an unresolved situation.

When Dispatching Protects Everyone

This chapter shows how dispatchers stand at the center of three human relationships simultaneously: the caller who speaks, the person the call concerns, and the officer whose safety depends on dispatcher information. Tri-subject asymmetry names that condition. What follows gives it a human face.

Lieutenant Pedro Marina spent 30 years on the streets of New Orleans, from narcotics enforcement to patrol to command, and he has never forgotten the dispatcher who worked one particular call. She remains at the console throughout the incident. She never fires a weapon, climbs a fence, or chases anyone through a residential backyard in the dark. Rather, she communicates clearly, acts precisely, and determines what happens to every human being with all her decisions, including the officer running through a darkened backyard toward two suspects he could not see. Her choices during that call illustrate what tri-subject asymmetry looks like when a dispatcher makes a sequence of decisions under pressure that keeps every person alive and accounted for throughout the entire situation.

He recounts what happened:

> I recall an incident in which the dispatcher made a difference for my safety as well as for the outcome of the incident. I was working a one-person car on the morning shift when a call came out about a possible burglary in progress in the Lakeview area. I was clear, so I responded to the call. As I was approaching the location, the dispatcher advised me to wait for backup. She immediately contacted a platoon sergeant for permission to preempt a two-person unit to back me up. The platoon sergeant consented and added that he would also proceed to the scene. Knowing that backup was en route, I exited my vehicle and proceeded to the address in question.
>
> The dispatcher then advised me to use caution. She had called the complainant and learned that the complainant lived across the street and had observed two white males, one wearing a black t-shirt and blue jeans, the other wearing a white t-shirt and brown cargo shorts, force the door open and enter the dwelling. As I approached the door, weapon in hand, I could hear noise coming from the house. I pushed the door wide open and observed the two males in question run out the back door into the backyard. I advised the dispatcher of what I had seen. She wasted no time calling for backup units to enter the house and meet me.
>
> I pursued the perpetrators into the backyard, calling for them to stop, when they jumped over a six-foot fence and out of sight. I advised the dispatcher that I had lost sight of the perpetrators when the sergeant arrived on scene and ordered some units to the street behind our location. As I climbed over the fence and took a hard fall on the other side, I heard a call to clear the channel. Two officers had spotted the men in question and were in hot pursuit. I limped through the side alley of the house behind onto the street, where I was able to catch a glimpse of the two perpetrators as they ran into another yard about a block away. The police pursuit continued as officers surrounded the block to contain the perpetrators.
>
> I finally limped all the way to the house when I was happy to see a K-9 unit warn everybody to stay out of the yard. Rudy, the K-9, was going to do his job. I stood by the front of the house, weapon in hand, as I heard the dog bark and the two perpetrators run toward me with Rudy in pursuit. The two perpetrators were tackled to the ground by

some 20 police officers, including me. As they were handcuffed, I could hear them asking for the location of Rudy. Rudy did not get his reward that day, as the K-9 officer held him back.

As the situation was secured, I returned to the scene of the crime to conduct the investigation, which was now labeled as a burglary. I figured that the investigation would be assigned to me since I was the first unit on scene. When I advised the dispatcher that I was back on the scene of the burglary and to notify the crime lab, the dispatcher asked me if I was all right and said that she was sending EMS to check me out. Apparently, she had heard me coughing and puffing after my fall from the back fence. I thanked her and declined EMS. All I had suffered was some dirt on my uniform.

As I looked back, I realized the important role the dispatcher played. She asked me to wait for backup, recognized the danger and sent backup, notified K-9, and finally checked on me to see if I was hurt and needed EMS.

From the moment the call was answered to the moment she sent EMS to check on an officer coughing after a fall he never reported, this dispatcher never stopped seeing three human beings simultaneously. She saw the complainant across the street watching two men force a door. She saw the suspects running through backyards in the dark. She saw the officer climbing a fence alone and tracked him through the radio silence that followed.

What she did was hold the entire situation in her mind and refuse to let any part of it drop. She coordinated backup before Marina reached the door, transmitted descriptions before he saw the suspects, called for containment before they cleared the fence, and checked on his body before he thought to check on it himself. Every decision she made protected someone.

The suspects were apprehended. No one sustained serious injury. The officer went home.

The Four-Question Framework: Making Decisions in Real Time

The dispatcher in the story above never stopped asking the right questions. Here is what those questions look like made explicit.

What Human Rights Are at Stake?

Every call implicates three sets of rights at once. The caller has rights to safety, dignity, privacy, and meaningful response. The person described or named in the call holds rights to dignity, presumption of innocence, and proportional response grounded in behavior. The officer pulling up to the scene holds rights to accurate information because it determines whether that officer enters a situation prepared with clarity or with a pre-formed narrative.

Skip this question and one of those perspectives collapses. A caller gets dismissed, a subject becomes a predefined threat, and an officer enters a scene without adequate situational awareness. Start here and all three remain visible long enough to guide the response.

How Does This Decision Protect One Person's Rights While Limiting Another's in the Same Moment?

Human rights protection happens in the dispatcher's actions. A dispatcher who listens without cutting off detail, records what the caller reports, and transmits that information with precision gives officers a clear account before they pull up. The tone keeps the caller engaged. The response matches what is happening. At times, it connects the caller to resources that address the conditions that produced the call in the first place.

These are the difference between rights existing on paper and a person experiencing them on the other end of the line.

Some situations require limitation of autonomy or privacy to prevent harm. A mental health crisis may require intervention that limits one's autonomy while still preserving human rights and proportional response. The question is whether those limitations match what the situation supports, or whether assumptions pushed them beyond what the situation required. When restrictions exceed necessity, they distort the situation for both the subject and the responding officer. The correction must occur while the call remains open, while adjustment remains possible.

What Does Agency Require?

Protocol covers routine calls that unfold in predictable patterns, such as a noise complaint that resolves after a warning or a minor traffic incident with no injuries. Real calls often move outside those patterns while the dispatcher gathers information. A burglary report may include only partial details, then expand as the caller describes movement inside the home. A medical call may begin as "someone feeling sick" and shift into signs of stroke or cardiac distress as questions narrow to fit the reality of the situation.

Some calls proceed immediately because the information is clear and complete at intake. Others require the dispatcher to pause dispatch, ask additional questions about what the caller sees, hears, and knows firsthand, and correct early assumptions before they decide the response. In certain situations, the dispatcher updates responding units as new facts develop, changes the assigned level of response, or holds units back until critical details stabilize. At other times, the dispatcher refuses to close a call too quickly when early descriptions conflict with later clarification, keeping the line open until the situation is properly defined.

Agency means seeing all three people clearly enough to act on what each of them needs.

How Would I Want to Be Treated?

This question anchors the framework in judgment formed at the dispatch center through repeated exposure to urgent calls. It demands fairness under pressure. The caller becomes a person whose urgency must be kept without distortion. The person in crisis becomes someone described without being reduced to a label. The officer becomes someone whose safety depends on the accurate transmission of details.

Would the words dispatched reflect what the dispatcher knows? Would the description give officers enough detail to understand what to expect at the scene?

The golden rule of doing to others what you would want done to you applies. Treat the caller, the subject of the call, and the police officer as you would want to be treated, as you would want your mother treated.

The Officer on the Other End

The four questions provide a framework, but frameworks don't work on the street. The people who apply them do. What that looks like from 30 years of field experience demands a different kind of witness. Chief Allen Hill of the University of Wisconsin-La Crosse Police Department spent decades watching what happens between the dispatch center and the scene, how a call leaves dispatch as description and arrives in the field as expectation.

> What stands out most to me over the course of my career is not one single call, but a pattern I saw again and again: by the time officers got to the scene, the posture had often already been set by the way the call came out of dispatch. Sometimes you could feel it immediately. Officers arrived expecting someone to be combative, dangerous, unstable, intoxicated, or suspicious before they had ever laid eyes on the person themselves. Sometimes that framing was accurate, but sometimes it was based on a caller's fear, assumptions, or shorthand description that had hardened into something more definitive by the time it reached the field. What struck me over the years was how much of that shaping power was invisible in the official record. The report would capture the officer's actions, the subject's behavior, and the final outcome, but it

rarely captured how the initial framing had already narrowed the range of possible responses before anyone got there.

That taught me something important: human rights policing begins long before the officer steps out of the squad. It begins with the dispatcher. It begins with the questions asked, the details emphasized, the uncertainty acknowledged or ignored, and the difference between passing along what is known versus what is assumed. A dispatcher can either create room for a measured and thoughtful response, or unintentionally close that room before anyone arrives. If a vague concern is presented as a threat, the call changes. If bias is passed forward as fact, the response changes. If the dispatcher slows down just enough to separate behavior from perception, that changes things too. In those few seconds before anyone reaches the scene, a dispatcher can help set the stage for dignity and restraint, or for unnecessary escalation.

What I also think gets overlooked is that human rights dispatching does not only affect the public. It affects officers too. Dispatchers are human beings, and like anyone else, they can develop frustrations, assumptions, loyalties, and biases. They may believe one officer is competent and another is careless. They may trust one officer's judgment and quietly doubt another's. They may have resentment from prior interactions, shift conflicts, personality clashes, or reputation. If that bias starts shaping tone, urgency, the completeness of information, officer-safety warnings, backup decisions, or the willingness to clarify critical details, then the dispatcher is not just influencing the call, but the officer's safety, dignity, and ability to do the job fairly. Human rights dispatching has to include the principle that officers, too, deserve impartiality, professionalism, transparency, and fair treatment from the person on the other end of the radio. Bias directed at an officer can be just as consequential as bias directed at a caller, because it can affect how the call is received, how the officer is supported, and what risks the officer walks into.

That is why I feel so strongly that dispatcher training must be rethought. We continue to place dispatchers in one of the most consequential roles in public safety, yet we often train them as though the job is primarily clerical or technical. It is not. Dispatchers are the first gatekeepers of state authority.

That authority demands the same scrutiny the dispatcher brings to every call.

Recognizing Your Own Biases

Every human being in the world is biased. Bias is a basic human tendency. It is also socially informed and culturally reinforced. It colors how people see and experience the world. Bias affects how journalists report the news, how sociologists construct theories that explain social phenomena, how politicians develop policy, and how media commentators frame reality itself. It also shapes how dispatchers hear calls, describe people, and determine how quickly a caller's account is translated into fact. Naming bias does not stop it from moving through experience, repetition, and the memory of prior calls.

Human rights dispatching requires noticing when bias begins to influence decisions within a call. A dispatcher listens, records, and sends information that determines how officers approach a scene. Expectation forms quickly, especially after repeated calls from the same address or neighborhood, and it continues into the next call. A caller who contacts the dispatch center repeatedly arrives with a history already written in the system from earlier calls. That history narrows attention, shortens patience, and strips detail from what gets recorded in the current call. The call defines the person before contact occurs.

The dispatcher interrupts that drift mid-call, writes what the caller says, and sends that information along instead of what the system assumed before. Bias shows most clearly in the call log. The words entered into the log continue into the next decisions. Labels such as erratic, manipulative, or frequent caller decide how the next dispatcher reads the call and how the next officer approaches the scene. Clear documentation records behavior and separates observation from assumption. It holds the caller's account in place, protects the person described from being reduced to the history of previous calls, and gives the officer a clean starting point for action.

Personal assumptions move through dispatch channels as facts. The dispatcher who notices that movement interrupts it before it impacts the three people whose human rights depend on what the dispatcher sends.

References

BBC News. 2016. "Charles Kinsey: 'I Still Got My Hands in the Air! Sir, Why Did You Shoot Me?'" *BBC News*, July 21, 2016. https://www.bbc.com/news/world-us-canada-36859305.

Durkheim, Émile. 1897. *Suicide: A Study in Sociology*. Translated by John A. Spaulding and George Simpson. New York: Free Press, 1951.

Fromm, Erich. 1955. *The Sane Society*. New York: Rinehart and Company.

Stoughton, Seth W. 2014. "Law Enforcement's 'Warrior' Problem." *Harvard Law Review* 128: 225–34.

Terrill, William, and Stephen D. Mastrofski. 2002. "Situational and Officer-Based Determinants of Police Coercion." *Justice Quarterly* 19 (2): 215–48. https://doi.org/10.1080/07418820200095221.

Chapter 5

Seven Calls

The Call That Changes Everything: Dispatcher Donna Choufani and Tia Hernlen

On the night of March 28, 2005, Julie and David Hernlen were murdered in their bedroom in Volusia County, Florida. Their 5-year-old daughter Tia woke to the sound of gunshots. She walked into her parents' bedroom, saw blood on the floor, and called 911.

A five-minute conversation followed that the Volusia County Sheriff's Office later released as part of the public record. The case drew news coverage. Tia Hernlen's name became known. Dispatcher Donna Choufani's name remained unknown.

During those five minutes, Choufani gathered what information she could and sent help toward the home. She asked Tia about a black lab named Lizzah, about a pink door her mother picked out, about school that week. She kept the child oriented to what was familiar while deputies headed toward the house. She did not lose the emergency in the details or the child inside it. She told Tia she is doing well and that she is wonderful. She told her she should be proud of herself. She stayed with her through each question and answer until help arrived.

The transcript shows what happens when dispatchers balance providing life-saving instruction and necessary compassion. Choufani listens and responds, adjusting her tone to the child's pace. She treats Tia as someone who can participate in her own survival, even at 5 years old. In that exchange, the dispatcher makes human rights operational rather than theoretical, as safety, dignity, and attention are expressed through the dispatcher's voice and response to the person on the other end of the line.

Transcript of 911 Call, Volusia County Sheriff's Office, March 28, 2005. Released publicly by the Volusia County Sheriff. Dispatcher: Donna Choufani. Caller: Tia Hernlen, age 5 (Volusia County Sheriff's Office 2005).

DOI: 10.4324/9781003583868-5

Operator: 911, what is your emergency?
Child: Um, hello.
Operator: Hello. Is everything OK?
Child: My mommy and daddy
Operator: Uh-huh.
Child: I think there is a bullet on the floor.
Operator: And what?
Child: And there is blood coming out of my dad's mouth, and he fell off the bed.
Operator: Let me get someone right over to you. Did you, did you go in your mommy and daddy's room?
Child: Uh-huh, and there is blood.
Operator: All over the place?
Child: Not all over. There's blood on the plant and blood on the floor.
Operator: Oh my goodness and you have your little doggie with you?
Child: And three cats.
Operator: And three cats too?
Child: Three cats and one dog.
Operator: OK, are you the only one there besides mommy and daddy?
Child: Well I said "Mommy" and "Daddy" and they didn't even answer.
Operator: OK, OK, what I want you to do honey. I want you to stay on the phone with me. What is your name?
Child: (tells operator her name)
Operator: Oh that is a very pretty name.
Child: (blocked out)
Operator: Oh, I'm so sorry, that is a beautiful name. What is your doggie's name?
Child: Lizzah
Operator: OK, and what made you wake up tonight?
Child: There was, I think I heard a gunshot.
Operator: You heard a gun?
Child: Yes, and I see a bullet lying on the floor. I think it's a bullet.
Operator: Really!
Child: Mmm-hmm
Operator: Who has a gun in the house?
Child: I don't see a gun but I'm scared.
Operator: Oh sweetheart! I will not let anything happen to you.
Child: Can you send a deputy down here?
Operator: I promise I will. And you're only 5 years old?
Child: Mmm-hmm

Operator: You are so smart for 5 years old. Wow! Are you off from school this week?
Child: Um, no, I go to school next year.
Operator: You do? Oh my gosh, you're not even in kindergarten yet?
Child: Nope.
Operator: Oh, what's your doggie's name?
Child: Lizzah
Operator: Lizzah, what kind of doggie is she?
Child: She's a lab.
Operator: Oh my God, I love those. Those are so beautiful. Is she a black lab or is she a yellow lab?
Child: A black lab.
Operator: Oh, you are so smart.
Child: With, um, brown eyes.
Operator: Oh my goodness, how old is she?
Child: She is like 3 years old, or, 2 years old, I don't really know.
Operator: Wow! You can remember for a really long time.
Child: Yup.
Operator: Oh my goodness. Was there anybody else in the house tonight besides you and mommy and daddy? Like an uncle or anything?
Child: No, there's no robber in the house.
Operator: OK, well I didn't think there would be a robber sweetheart. Did you have anybody staying over the night with you guys tonight?
Child: Mmm-hmm
Operator: OK. So the doors are all locked? Where are you in the house?
Child: Well, I was in my room sleeping till I heard a noise shot and it woke me up.
Operator: Oh my goodness. What part of the house are you in now?
Child: I'm in the one, it's yellow, all yellow house, of green, green with it, a little bit of green, and a pink door.
Operator: Oh my goodness, that sounds really cool. Did you pick out the pink door?
Child: Um, no, my mom picked out the door.
Operator: I bet that is beautiful. Does mommy and daddy have a car in the driveway?
Child: Mmm-hmm, two cars.
Operator: Two cars? What kind of cars do they have?
Child: Umm, my mom has a Toyota.
Operator: What color is that Toyota?
Child: It's um red.

Operator: Red? OK, what kind of car does daddy have?
Child: He has a Jeep. It's black and . . .
Operator: OK, listen to me. Is your phone the type that you can take with you and walk around?
Child: Um, this . . .
Operator: There should be an officer at your front door. I need for you to take your phone with you and walk over to the door and open it for me, OK? And I will stay on the phone with you, OK?
Child: But um . . .
Operator: I will not hang up.
Child: I'm naked.
Operator: Oh, well do you want to grab a towel or something? I don't think the officer's going to care baby. We just want to make sure that mommy and daddy are OK, all right?
Child: Mmm-hmm.
Operator: Grab a blanket or something. Stay on the phone with me, stay on the phone, alright?
Child: OK.
Operator: My name is Donna, by the way. You are doing a wonderful job, wonderful job.
Child: And I know what to do for (incoherent)
Operator: You did great!
Child: I knew.
Operator: You were wonderful, absolutely wonderful. You should be very proud of yourself.
Child: I'm to the door, I'm unlocking it.
Operator: OK, you let me know when the officer talks to you.
Officer: (background) You talking to the dispatcher? OK, tell her I'm here now and you can hang up.
Operator: Bye sweetheart.
Child: Um, he's here.
Operator: OK sweetheart, you be good, OK? Bye-bye.

What Donna Choufani Did

Choufani dispatched units within the first 30 seconds. Everything that followed served the dual purposes of gathering the information officers needed and keeping Tia Hernlen anchored in the moment.

The questions about Lizzah the black lab, the pink door, and the Toyota in the driveway were not simply diversions but tactics to manage the emergency. A 5-year-old standing in a house where her parents had just been killed needed something safe and familiar on the other end of the line, and Choufani gave her that connection to guide the child through this event.

She also reflects the child's capability back to her through direct affirmation. "You are so smart for 5 years old." "You were wonderful, absolutely wonderful. You should be very proud of yourself." These statements acknowledge what Tia is doing. She woke up alone, found the phone, dialed 911, and stayed on the line. Choufani names that plainly so the child can hear it and feel connected to something.

In that exchange, dispatching becomes sustained attention under pressure. It holds two demands at once: the requirements of the call and the condition of the caller. Choufani manages both simultaneously through instruction and reassurance.

Theory and Practice

Theory and practice must tango together. Chapter 4 set out the framework of human rights dispatching. What follows shows how that framework holds under pressure. Donna Choufani shows one example of what it looks like when a dispatcher gets it right.

The calls here test patience, expose bias, and force uncomfortable reckonings with the power dispatchers hold. Some arrive wrapped in the language of concern but bring a history of suspicion that turned to harm. Others come barely audible, a woman whispering from a locked bathroom while the person who hurt her sleeps down the hall. Others happen as routine radio requests from officers who expect compliance and hold the institutional power to punish its absence. None announce their difficulty in advance.

These calls unfold in ways no manual anticipates, requiring technical skill, moral clarity, interpretive insight, and the courage to exercise judgment beyond routine. The dispatcher faces scrutiny in every scenario, and every decision made under pressure tests human rights obligations alongside everything else.

Perfection is an impossible standard. People make mistakes. Bias slips through despite the best intentions. Patience falters under the accumulated strain of a profession that asks people to absorb the worst of human experience without carrying it afterward. What matters is the willingness dispatchers bring to recognize the human rights implications in every call, to make choices that move beyond procedure, and to treat ethical responsibility as a practice that institutions often ignore.

Every scenario in this chapter asks the dispatcher to hold three distinct human beings in mind at once: the officer responding to the call, the caller reaching out, and the person the call concerns. These interests do not always align, and the dispatcher must navigate that tension without the luxury of deliberation, under institutional pressure to process the call and move on quickly. No other role determines what each person affected by the call will encounter when help finally arrives.

The four principles, the seven rights, and the five questions in Chapter 4 form the ethical foundation of human rights dispatching. What follows tests them one call at a time.

Scenario I: The Frequent Caller – Human Rights, Agency, and the Blasé Attitude

The Number You Already Know

The dispatcher recognizes certain numbers the moment they appear on the screen, drawing on prior calls, past reports, and unresolved outcomes. The frequent caller occupies a peculiar position in emergency communication, where policy treats each call as new even as the record shows continuity. This tension within the dispatch center remains unexamined. A dispatcher who sighs before answering renders a judgment before a word is spoken. The blasé attitude cuts deepest with frequent callers.

The Sixteenth Call

It is 2:14 in the morning. The number appears on the screen. The dispatcher recognizes it before the first ring finishes. Fifteen calls in the past month, all from the same fourth-floor apartment in a building flagged as a frequent contact address. The prior calls sit in the log, a record the dispatcher reads before answering. Noise complaints are unsubstantiated. Reports of a neighbor watching through windows are unconfirmed. One welfare check found the caller agitated but unharmed. The system marked each call as unfounded and moved on.

Upon answering the call, the dispatcher hears a voice pulled tight with the effort of holding itself steady, the specific flatness of someone who has braced for dismissal. A woman, middle-aged by the sound of her voice, speaks carefully, choosing words the way a person chooses steps on ice. Someone is outside her window again, she says. She can hear them on the fire escape. The street noise of the city filters through the line, a distant siren, the low hum of traffic, and beneath it, the quality of silence that fills a small apartment at two in the morning when a person is too afraid to move.

She knows how this sounds. The hesitation in her voice retains the memory of prior dispatchers who have heard these same words and treated them as routine. She braces for the sigh, the clipped tone, the suggestion that she call back if something happens. What the dispatcher does in the next few seconds determines everything. The caller has the right to respected, to be heard, and to access emergency services. Those rights remain, regardless of how many times that number has appeared on the screen.

The dispatcher returns to the first question and asks what is happening right now. The caller answers in her own words, which remain the center of the call. The record of prior calls stays in the background as context. The dispatcher hears the woman speaking at 2:14 in the morning. Her account stands on its own, separate from the calls that came before it.

Prior Calls Provide Context, Not Conclusions

Patterns inform judgment but do not replace it. A person who calls 15 times about a neighbor watching through the window may call a 16th time because something has changed. If a dispatcher decides what the call is before the caller finishes speaking, that decision narrows what can be heard and what can be acted on. The call becomes a repetition instead of a report. When that happens, the risk is not in the caller's history. It is in the dispatcher's certainty.

Why People Call 15 Times

People call 15 times because the institutions around them fail to resolve the conditions that drive them to seek help. They move through intake desks, waiting rooms, and offices where access depends on what they can produce: an insurance card, a stable address, a form completed without error. A clinic visit ends when insurance coverage cannot be verified. A missed bus turns an appointment into another absence recorded in a file. A caseworker logs the visit, enters it into a system, and closes the case while the conditions that produced the visit remain unchanged.

That pattern reflects social exclusion and marginalization. It reflects a social order that extracts labor, time, and personal information while withholding care, attention, and recognition from those who cannot meet its terms. People who cannot meet those terms return to the few points of contact still available. The apartment stays quiet except for the refrigerator cycling and pipes shifting in the walls. The phone becomes the only way to break a silence that grows heavier over time. When every other door closes, 911 remains open, and the dispatcher becomes the only human voice available. Repetition wears on the people answering the calls, but it also points to conditions that remain unchanged because no system stays with them long enough to resolve them. Responsibility sits with the institutions that record contact and close cases while the conditions continue outside the record.

Starting Without the Sigh

The dispatcher answers without the sigh and sets aside what the screen suggests before the call connects. They acknowledge prior calls refuse to let it decide this call. The dispatcher asks what is happening tonight, in this apartment, on the fire escape, at this very moment.

The woman describes a sound, something scraping along the metal grating outside her bedroom window. She admits, almost reluctantly, that it frightened her enough to call. The dispatcher listens beyond the record and hears a woman alone at two in the morning, afraid, reaching toward the phone. The dispatcher asks her to stay on the phone and guides her to check the sound only when she feels ready to move.

She crosses the apartment slowly. The dispatcher stays with her, listening to her footsteps, the creak of floorboards, the soft pull of a curtain. No one is there. A branch moves against the fire escape in the wind. Yet, the fear remains. It remains in the uncertainty felt in the time between what she heard and what she found. The dispatcher feels that uncertainty and keeps her on the line.

The dispatcher asks how safe she feels. She answers that she feels safe, but her voice contains something heavier than the words. It carries the strain of living with this kind of fear for a long time.

She says she needs someone to talk to. This admission makes the situation clear. No immediate threat remains. What remains is isolation, steady and unaddressed. A woman learns that the dispatcher is often the only voice she reaches at 2:14 in the morning when fear becomes too large to feel alone.

The dispatcher offers an explanation, simple and plausible: a branch against the fire escape, wind moving through the alley. The explanation gives the experience a form she can hold onto afterward. The dispatcher provides a non-emergency support line, a resource suited to what the call has become. The call ends with direction toward help that fits the situation.

Documentation as Dignity

What dispatchers record in this situation matters as much as how they handle the call. The entry notes that the caller reports sounds on the fire escape, she checks and finds a branch moving in the wind, and she remains unsettled after the inspection. The record avoids collapsing the call into a familiar label. It brings forward the details so that the next dispatcher who sees the number confronts a situation that remains unresolved.

A referral for social services follow-up extends the response beyond the call and into what surrounds it. It acknowledges a need that does not end when the call does. Documentation becomes the final step of the interaction in the system, and when it is written thoughtfully, it influences how the next point of contact understands what happened here and what may still be happening.

Resisting the Blasé Attitude

The number appears on the screen at 2:14 in the morning and the history loads behind it. The dispatcher recognizes the pattern before the call connects. Prior notes sit in the record, but the call itself does not come from those notes. It comes from a fourth-floor apartment, from a woman alone in the dark, from a sound outside her window that makes her reach for the phone again.

That is the only call that exists right now. The dispatcher who meets it on its own terms and asks what is happening treats it as new, even when the record is old. In doing so, the dispatcher preserves something frequent callers lose first, the chance to be heard without concern of what came before. Sometimes the situation changes. Sometimes it does not. The only way to know is to listen long enough to find out.

Scenario II: Language, Rights, and the Limits of Understanding

Immigrant Communities

Emergency communication depends on shared language. Dispatchers answer calls expecting to understand the language being spoken well enough to identify what is happening and send help. In cities with immigrant communities and neighborhoods in constant transition, multiple languages are spoken on the same streets, in homes, shops, and public spaces. At times, the dispatcher does not understand the language the caller is using. The caller may speak a language the dispatcher does not know or shift between languages within the same sentence. In New York, for example, many people describe this shifting between English and Spanish as "Spanglish." Speech may arrive in fragments, repetition, or urgent phrases that do not form a clear request. The dispatcher listens for usable information, like names, locations, repeated words, and signs of urgency that can be acted on. Training prepares dispatchers for speed, radio procedure, and structured communication. It does not always prepare them for calls that exceed shared linguistic understanding. The call still proceeds. What happens after depends on whether enough is understood to identify the situation and send help.

The Call

It is 11:23 at night in a third-floor apartment in a neighborhood where bodegas stay open late and cumbia drifts through screen doors in summer. The line opens and a woman's voice breaks through in Spanish, words spilling over each other, fractured by terror, too fast for even a fluent speaker to follow. The dispatcher speaks English. What comes through is alarm, a voice stretched to its limit, breath pulled in sharp bursts, words collapsing into each other the way speech does when the body moves beyond control. Behind her voice a man shouts, words sharp and close, and something heavy hits the floor with a sound that travels through the phone like a fist through drywall. In the apartment a child cries quietly and muffled, contained.

The pitch of her voice signals terror. Her breathing stays uneven. Her voice does not settle long enough to form clear structure. A child cries in the background – a small, contained sound that marks vulnerability inside whatever unfolds on the other side of the line. The first question surfaces immediately. What is happening right now. The sounds answer it. What happens afterward depends on what the dispatcher does in the next few seconds.

When the Line Goes Dead

The dispatcher tries once, then again, asking for English, shifting phrasing, listening for any response that might make the call usable. No interpreter joins the call. No alternative follows. The line goes quiet. The dispatcher tells the caller to find someone who speaks English and call back.

On the other end, a woman stands in her kitchen holding a phone in both hands, the man's voice still in the apartment behind her, and the dial tone replacing the voice that was there seconds earlier.

She hesitates before dialing, longer than the call itself, because everything her life has taught her about institutions, uniforms, authority, and what happens when people like her ask for help pushes back against each number she presses. She calls because she believes someone can help her through the most dangerous moment of her night. The dispatcher answers, tries twice, and sends her back into the room alone. Another caller in another context would have received immediate dispatch. Instead, she bears the consequence of a system that does not respond to her language.

The Courage to Dial 911

Many callers with limited English hesitate on the phone for a long time before speaking. They come from places where a uniform at the door means punishment, where asking an institution for help puts families at risk, where invisibility becomes the only reliable form of safety. Dialing 911 requires a courage the dispatcher on the other end rarely fully understands. This woman presses each digit knowing the system may fail her. She calls anyway because the alternative seems somehow worse.

Verstehen Without Words

The dispatcher who stays on the line reads the call through everything language fails to convey. Panic moves through pitch and breath and the rhythm of speech collapses under pressure the way water moves through a crack, finding every opening, filling every available space. A child crying in the background tells the dispatcher something precise about who else occupies the apartment and how long the danger has been building. An object hitting the floor signals proximity and force. The half-second pause before her voice drops, the moment the man's shouting stops and the apartment goes briefly and terrifyingly quiet, these reveal what vocabulary alone fails to communicate.

Verstehen, the disciplined effort to understand another person's experience from within the conditions they are living through, becomes most necessary when language fails. In dispatch, it works through tone, rhythm, and the texture of a voice under pressure. When language is not shared, understanding forms from fragments of speech, timing, and reaction. This type of understanding recognizes another person's experience within conditions they did not choose. In that recognition, response becomes possible, and from response, protection can follow. The emergency remains real regardless of the caller's language.

Police. Fire. Ambulance.

The dispatcher slows their speech, reduces volume, and holds a steady cadence so clarity becomes the primary signal across the line. They speak clearly and slowly, police, fire, ambulance, words worn smooth by a thousand emergencies in a hundred languages. They listen for anything recognizable, a street number, a fragment of an address, a name, a sound from outside the window that might place the apartment on a map.

Dispatchers who know even a handful of words in the languages their city speaks use them. Effort crosses the line even when fluency does not. The caller does not need the dispatcher to speak her language. She needs to hear someone trying to reach her, that the silence after each question shows attention, that the steady voice on the other end will remain.

A workable address moves units even when everything else remains unclear. The dispatcher works with whatever arrives and acts on it.

Staying on the Line

The dispatcher stays on the line. The voice on the other end continues, trembling and afraid and still holding on. Presence matters. Every second the dispatcher remains communicates what the call makes real, that this caller possesses human rights regardless of the language she speaks, that her emergency counts, and that someone answers her.

Three minutes later, a translator joins the call. The situation comes into focus. A domestic violence incident unfolds. A 6-year-old is inside the apartment. The address places the call on the west side of the block between two intersections the dispatcher can locate on the map. Units move. When the woman hears that help is coming, her voice steadies. The language barrier no longer blocks what needs to be understood. She stayed on the line because someone on the other side stayed first.

A Choice About Whose Safety Matters

Dispatchers in urban settings routinely take calls from multilingual households. Language barriers are a routine part of every shift. Dispatchers unprepared for those barriers decide whose emergencies count producing uneven outcomes. The difference shows up in how quickly help moves, how clearly information travels, and how much uncertainty a dispatcher reveals.

Each dispatcher decides whether to close that divide or resist it. They send help on partial information when waiting for certainty would take too long. They treat the emergency as real in the moment it reaches them, and they work it with the same urgency and attention they bring to every call, regardless of language or how clearly the situation comes through. The woman on the third floor pressed each digit knowing the system might fail her. The dispatcher who stayed on the line gave her, for that night, a reason to trust that it would hold.

Scenario III: Walking While Black – Agency, Bias, and the Construction of Suspicion

Who Gets to Belong

Few calls show the dispatcher's role more clearly than those in which someone requests police response for a person whose only action is walking or simply occupying space. The call arrives as a concern framed as an appeal to safety and neighborhood protection, but beneath that "concern" is a history of prior calls and responses that pre-determines how the situation gets interpreted. Walking, standing, or simply existing in certain places draws scrutiny and threat along racial lines formed through long-standing practices that have been repeated consistently throughout history. This translates to whether emergency communication protects rights or turns ordinary presence into a reason for intervention.

The Performance of Concern

It's a Saturday afternoon in late October, the kind of cool clear day that brings people outside. A Black man walks down a tree-lined street in a predominantly white neighborhood, hands in his jacket pockets, moving at the unhurried pace of someone with nowhere to be and no need to hurry. He glances at houses the way anyone observes the world around them while on a walk, taking in the street, moving through public space as he moves through any other.

A woman watches him from behind a curtain on the second floor of her house. She picks up the phone.

When the dispatcher answers, the caller's voice bears a tremor that does work before the complaint fully forms. She describes a Black man in a hoodie moving slowly down the street, glancing at houses, and she wants the dispatcher to confirm that this warrants concern. The racial description contains the full historical weight of the complaint. Decades of redlining, exclusionary housing policies, and concentrated economic pressure produced this neighborhood, and those same forces taught the people inside it to read Black presence as intrusion – the invisible lines of American apartheid. The caller frames the man's walk as suspicious and waits for the dispatcher to convert that private judgment into something official, something with a badge and a car and the authority to make him explain himself.

When Language Moves Bias Forward

The dispatcher confirms the description and dispatches officers on a suspicious person call. The call moves as routine. The routine is the problem. A Black male in a hoodie is walking through the neighborhood, caller considers the subject suspicious. Those words travel to officers before they see anything and build what they expect to find. A man exercising the constitutional right to walk on a public street becomes a potential threat. He carries his groceries and phone, or perhaps nothing at all, walking the same street a white resident walked an hour earlier without generating a single call, and the presumption of innocence that white pedestrian walking without thinking about it evaporates the moment the dispatcher says the word suspicious next to a description without any observable crime.

The dispatcher who pushes the call forward without interrogating it participates in a long history of prejudice and discrimination embedded in social practice. The dispatcher who pauses and asks what rights are at stake in this situation applies human rights principles, including the right to life and security of person, that routine practice obscures. A man walks down a public street. That is all that is happening, the entire factual content of this call.

The History Inside the Call

This call brings centuries into the dispatch center. Slave patrols stopped Black people who moved without authorization. Vagrancy laws criminalized Black mobility after emancipation. Decades of residential segregation produced predominantly white neighborhoods where Black presence reads as intrusion, a dynamic Du Bois documented more than a century ago (Du Bois 1903). The caller did not invent any of this. Her nervousness feels genuine because American society cultivated it deliberately, training generations to associate Blackness with danger and disorder. Stanley Cohen identified the folk devil as the figure a society creates to bear its anxieties and absorb its fears (Cohen 1972/2011). This call constructs one, loading the man walking down the street with the accumulated discomfort of a neighborhood that decided he does not belong there before he turns the corner.

Asking the Question That Ends the Complaint

The dispatcher asks a question. What has this person done? Has he approached any property, tested any door, threatened anyone, or committed any observable violation? The caller answers each question in the same way. The man walked past houses. He glanced at buildings lining a public street. He did what people do when they walk through a neighborhood, and someone called the police.

Then the caller says something that clarifies what is driving the concern. They rarely see people like him in this area. In that admission, the basis of the call becomes clear. The dispatcher explains that walking through a neighborhood is lawful, that public space is shared, and that only specific observed actions justify a police response. The caller's discomfort does not meet that threshold.

When a Response Goes Out Anyway

When the caller insists and a response still goes out, the way that response is framed determines whether the man walking gets to exercise his basic rights to simply exist and move through a public street without interference or harassment. The dispatcher establishes that a man is walking in the area, that no crime has been reported or observed, that no property has been touched, and that no threat is present. The response goes out as a welfare check. The officer receives a clear legal basis for the call, reasonable suspicion is not present, and the man on that sidewalk has the right to be there.

That framing shapes how the officer approaches the street when the patrol car pulls up. The dispatcher who codes this as a suspicious person call and the dispatcher who codes it as a welfare check send two different instructions. One treats lawful presence as something to manage as risk. The other treats it as something to protect.

What the dispatcher writes into the record extends that protection beyond the call itself. The entry notes that the caller reported a person walking, that no criminal activity occurred, that the dispatcher explained the legality of occupying public space, and that the response went out as a welfare check. That record demonstrates how the call was read and how it was resolved. A supervisor reviewing it months later sees a documented moment where the dispatcher identified the nature of the call and responded accordingly.

The Refusal to Launder Prejudice

Philippe Bourgois documented the United States as a country organized through geographic and opportunity-based separation, where structural inequality and housing segregation determine who belongs in certain areas and who gets treated as an intruder for entering them (Bourgois 2003). The stops that follow calls like this land on a man who walked down a public street on a Saturday afternoon with his hands in his pockets and his mind on wherever he was going. The dispatcher who sent that stop forward participated in something older and larger than any single call. The dispatcher who refused participated in something different, something the man walking home will never know happened, and something the record will travel forward long after both have moved on.

Scenario IV: The Locked Bathroom – Crisis, Framing, and the Difference Between Help and Force

Words Build the World Officers Walk Into

Every word the dispatcher chooses sets the situation in motion before officers leave the station. Framing a person as an armed subject leads toward a tactical standoff. Framing the same person as someone in crisis with access to a firearm leads toward a response aimed at a human being in distress. The language moves ahead of the response through the briefing and into the street, where it influences how officers stand, how they approach the door, and how they make contact. What begins as phrasing becomes posture by the time hands rise to knock on the door.

A Mother's Voice

It is 9:47 on a Tuesday night and the house has gone quiet in the way that houses go quiet when something terrible sits just behind a closed door. A mother stands in the hallway of her home, one hand pressed flat against the bathroom wall, the other holding her phone so tightly her knuckles go pale. On the other side of the door, her 17-year-old son sits on the tile floor with a gun in his lap, crying in the way people do when they run out of options. She can hear him. Each sob moves through the wood and lands somewhere beneath her ribs.

She calls 911 because she has nowhere else to turn. She understands, the way only a mother can who has tracked her child's fragility across years of medication adjustments and hospitalizations with narrow recoveries, that the next few minutes will decide whether her son lives or dies. She knows something the dispatcher cannot see. Police encounters with psychiatric distress sometimes end in death, and calling for help has its own risk if the words go wrong. She does more than report an emergency. She trusts a system that can save her son's life or, if the framing goes wrong, place it in danger.

The Label of the Armed Subject

The dispatcher listens as the mother describes the situation behind that door. Her son lives under intense and acute pressure. He has no history of violence toward others. The pain turns inward, always inward, and the only person at risk is him.

Within seconds, the call system translates her words into operational categories. The son becomes an armed subject. The bathroom becomes a barricaded location. The event escalates to high risk. These labels retain a technical function, but they strip away context. They remove the detail that determines how the situation unfolds and replace it with a shorthand that signals threat to responders trained to deal with danger.

Officers arrive with a posture already set by that framing, moving to assert authority over a situation their briefing has defined as dangerous. That posture can disrupt the fragile balance inside that bathroom. His mother called because she understood something no protocol captures, and the system recorded her words and replaced them with a category. That replacement can get her son killed.

Structural Failures and the Dispatcher's Refusal

The deinstitutionalization movement of the 1960s closed psychiatric facilities without building the community alternatives it promised, and emergency services absorbed responsibility by default. Jails now hold more people with serious mental illness than psychiatric hospitals do (Rogers, McNiel, and Binder 2019). News coverage and television drama reinforced the association between psychiatric conditions and violence across decades, training responders to see danger before suffering.

Dispatchers work within those structural failures. But each dispatcher still makes choices in how they describe a call and what they emphasize when they pass it forward. Those choices affect how officers read the scene, how they approach a door, and what they expect to find on the other side.

Language becomes one of the only tools available at that point. It can tilt a response toward compassion that protects human rights, or toward confrontation that treats distress as threat.

The Mother as Partner

The dispatcher matches the mother's urgency and slows the pace, guiding the conversation through questions that only someone who knows the child's daily life can answer. She knows her son in ways that go far beyond what any intake form captures, and each answer she gives affects how help arrives, and whether it arrives as help at all.

The dispatcher asks who else is in the house. She lives alone with him. The question helps protect the responding officers and clarifies that the only person at immediate risk is the son inside the bathroom. Can she still hear him? Yes, he cries softly. The dispatcher treats that sound as presence, proof that he is still reachable, that intervention still has somewhere to land.

What happened recently? He stopped his medication two weeks ago. That timing points toward a known risk that follows untreated depression. Has he ever been violent toward others? No, his suffering turns inward. Has this happened before? Yes. She pulled him back once already, which means there is a history of recovery to work from.

Each question the dispatcher asks collects a fact and recovers a person. Each answer opens a door, and more options, and the dispatcher goes through every one of them, because behind the locked bathroom door sits a boy who remains reachable and who can recover, and reaching him begins with the dispatcher.

The Dispatch

Officers go out quietly, no sirens. The dispatcher instructs the mother to meet them outside so they know who they encounter before knocking on the door.

The call goes out as a mental health crisis. A 17-year-old male is locked in a bathroom with a firearm. His mother waits outside, cooperative and alert. He has a history of severe depression. He stopped his medication two weeks ago. He survived a previous attempt after she intervened.

Officers receive instructions to approach calmly and prioritize communication over control. A Crisis Intervention Team response is activated.

Every officer moving toward that house receives what the label armed subject fails to deliver: a human being in need, someone reachable and responsive, someone whose mother stands on the porch in the dark because she trusted the dispatcher to get the words right.

The language builds their posture before knocking. It informs how officers move through the hallway and how they position themselves at the door. It affects what they believe they are about to encounter. It determines whether the boy behind that door survives the night.

Verstehen in Practice

The dispatcher never tells the mother to calm down. Verstehen, that disciplined effort to understand the world from inside another person's experience, begins with questions and builds toward understanding the system would not reach on its own.

Can you still hear him? That question hands the mother something to do with her terror and makes her a partner. Where she hears crying as despair, the dispatcher names it as presence, proof that her son remains reachable. That shift, small in words but not in effect, steadies her enough to answer what comes next.

Each question draws out more of the person behind the crisis. The medication, the earlier survival, the diagnosis, the suffering that turns inward, each detail adds to a picture that will travel with responders to the door.

Words Determine What Officers Find

Mental health crises become dangerous when responders arrive with the wrong picture. The difference between an armed subject and a young man in crisis sits in how the situation is described. That description shapes posture, influences tactics, and affects how officers move through the hallway and what they expect at the door. It follows them to the moment someone speaks through the wood to the boy sitting on the bathroom floor.

The mother stands in that hallway with her hand against the wall and her phone pressed to her ear, trusting that the words moving through the line toward her son's door will reach it in a form that reflects what is behind the door. The dispatcher who understands what those words will set in motion sends them forward with care and precision. On this day, that choice protects a boy's human rights, beginning with his right to life.

Scenario V: Safety, Autonomy, and the Knowledge Victims Bring

Who Knows Best

Domestic calls involve a level of complexity that emergency response systems were not designed to capture. The person in danger often knows which actions lower risk and which make things worse, shaped by repeated exposure to the same person, the same patterns, sometimes over years. That knowledge comes from reading threat in the situation the caller presents, in a way no protocol can fully reproduce.

When a dispatcher answers a call from someone whispering in fear, two obligations sit in the line at once. One points toward intervention when violence is present. The other requires attention to what the caller says about how to move safely in that moment

The Moment That Determines Survival

It is 2:17 in the morning and the house sits completely still. In the locked bathroom of a second-floor apartment, a woman crouches on the cold tile floor with her back against the bathtub and her phone pressed so close to her mouth that her breath fogs the screen. Her left cheekbone throbs where his fist connected an hour ago. Down the hall, she can hear him breathing while sleeping, the long slow rhythm of someone who exhausted himself and went down hard. She has been listening to that rhythm for 40 minutes, measuring it, reading it the way she reads everything about him, with the precise attention of someone whose safety depends on getting the reading right.

She dials 911. Her voice stays low, almost swallowed by the room, and the dispatcher leans in to hear. Her boyfriend hit her tonight. You can hear the fear in her words, and its deliberate calculation. He is asleep now. She asks for no sirens, no sudden knock, no lights breaking the windows. She has learned what a loud entrance can trigger. She tries to describe both what happened and what might happen next if the response is handled without care. She asks for protection while also trying to influence how it arrives, and the dispatcher must decide whether to incorporate that knowledge or default to routine response.

The Help That Escalates

The dispatcher hears the whispering, registers the assault, catches the warning that waking him will make everything worse. Standard procedure classifies the call into predefined risk categories. Domestic violence. High risk. Officers respond with lights and sirens, and the street outside fills with the familiar choreography of emergency response.

Sirens and lights exist for good reasons. Calls involving intimate partners rank among the most dangerous situations officers encounter. Rapid response developed over decades in response to cases where hesitation cost lives, in a time when domestic violence was often treated as a private matter. That history matters.

But she learned things the dispatch system does not know. She learned how he reacts when startled from sleep, how humiliation turns quickly into rage, how the stillness in the room holds him in place for the moment. Her knowledge comes from years of close attention to someone she has learned to read the way people read weather.

A squad car turns onto the block. Light spills through the window. The engine idles at the curb. He wakes and the stillness breaks. Before anyone establishes control, the scene unravels. She gets assaulted again in the same room where the response meant to protect her is still unfolding.

What She Brings to the Phone

Her hesitation before dialing comes from experience. Mandatory arrest policies removed officer discretion with the intention of ensuring that domestic violence calls were taken seriously, but they also changed what happens after the call. For some callers, an arrest can mean losing income, housing, or immigration stability. In other situations, both people in the home risk being taken into custody, including the person who called for help.

Years of calls that were minimized, misunderstood, or treated as routine built a kind of caution that appears in a single moment. She has experienced what can happen when the response goes the wrong way. She presses each digit anyway, because whatever she is facing inside the apartment is worse than the uncertainty of calling.

Double Consciousness in Crisis

She holds two realities at once while she whispers into the phone. Terror from the person who hurt her tonight pulses through her chest. Alongside it sits another fear, quieter but persistent, about what the response she just triggered might bring. She wonders whether she will be believed, whether she will be judged for staying, whether the call meant to protect her will make things worse. Du Bois described double consciousness as the experience of seeing oneself through one's own eyes and simultaneously through the eyes of a system that has already rendered its judgment (Du Bois 1903). On nights like this, that double vision sharpens into something acute. One kind of danger is in the room with her. Another is in what happens after she dials.

The dispatcher slows the pace of the exchange. The voice on the line stays low, and the dispatcher meets it there. The goal is simple. Keep her talking long enough to understand what is happening and what she needs next. She answers with precision. He is asleep in the bedroom down the hall. She is in a locked bathroom with an injury to her face. She knows where he is and what he does when awakened.

The dispatcher builds the next step from that information. Can she leave the house safely and meet officers outside before he wakes?, The question opens a path that standard response would often close before it is considered.

The Dispatch

Officers go out on a Code 3 with instructions to approach without sirens and park down the block. The suspect is asleep in the bedroom. The woman is in the bathroom with a facial injury and will leave the house to meet them before he wakes. Sudden movement or noise risks triggering him, and officers shift immediately to emergency entry if anything changes. Each instruction the dispatcher sends draws directly from her account, her knowledge of the person in the bedroom, and her assessment of what keeps the situation stable.

The dispatcher keeps the line open as she moves through the house, maintaining a steady voice through the most dangerous part of the night. Each step coordinated and each sound accounted for. She reaches the officers safely, and the dispatcher asks where she can go and whether she wants an advocate to stay with her, because safety extends beyond the moment officers arrive. Then the dispatcher tells her she was brave to call. Those words may matter later, returning in some future moment when she needs to remember that someone, at least once, understood what it cost her to pick up the phone.

Documentation as Protection

The dispatcher records her request for a silent approach, her fear of escalation, and the tactical adjustments made while maintaining Code 3 priority. Each step of the quiet exit gets documented, each decision that prevents the situation from fracturing, each moment where her knowledge guides the response. That record matters beyond this call.

The next dispatcher who picks up a call from her address reads something different from a standard domestic violence history. They read a situation already in motion, including specific information about what reduces danger in that household. Responders arrive with that knowledge in hand. What she said, and what the dispatcher did with it, remain visible in the file that follows her into the next call.

Protection and Autonomy

She knows her home at two in the morning, in a way the dispatcher cannot know from the other side of the line. She is aware of how a voice moves through the walls, how a slammed door travels through each room, how the silence of his sleep differs from the silence that means he is listening. When she explains that a loud or forceful approach will provoke violence, she gives the dispatcher knowledge beyond any protocol or training manual. The dispatcher who receives that knowledge and adjusts the response turns procedure into protection.

She will remember how help arrived on this night, moving quietly, following her lead, speaking at her pace. That memory returns later in the moment she stands in the kitchen and decides whether to reach for the phone.

Scenario VI: Sleeping in Public – Poverty, Visibility, and the Right to Exist

Debris or Human Being

It is 4:43 in the morning and the city moves in that specific pre-dawn quiet when the last bars have closed and the first delivery trucks have not yet turned onto the block. In the recessed doorway of a closed hardware store on a commercial street, a man sleeps with his back against the locked door and a canvas bag tucked beneath his head. His jacket is thin for the temperature. His boots are held together with electrical tape at the toe. He breathes slowly and deeply, the sleep of someone who learned long ago to sleep wherever the night allows. He threatens no one, blocks nothing, and rests in the only space available to him.

A business owner walking past on his way to open his shop two blocks down sees the man and reaches for his phone. He wants him gone. The dispatcher answers and inherits a decision that begins the moment the call connects, whether emergency communication treats a sleeping man as a public safety problem or turns one person's discomfort into official action against another person's exhausted body.

The Authority the Dispatcher Inherits

Law enforcement has the authority to define who belongs in public space, who may rest, and who must keep moving. When the call reaches the dispatcher, that authority passes into their hands. What they do with it determines what the man sleeping in the doorway will encounter when the city wakes up around him.

The Cycle of Futility

Standard procedure sends an officer to the sidewalk. The man is nudged awake. He blinks against the streetlight, gathers himself and his possessions, and moves on to the next block. The dispatcher logs a trespassing complaint, and the shift continues.

An hour later, or the next night, another call comes from another business on another block. The same sequence repeats. The man moves again, tired, carrying everything he owns, another doorway lost, another block added to the route he is forced to trace through a city that offers no place to go.

Each compelled move erodes human rights, the right to rest, the right to safety, the right to exist somewhere without being told to exist elsewhere. People with homes sit on benches and rest in parks and nobody dials 911. People without homes face enforcement for the same acts.

How Poverty Became a Policing Problem

For most of human history people did not need to justify their presence through a lease. They claimed space, slept where the land allowed, and built shelter from what surrounded them. Public areas existed to be occupied without justification. Over centuries, housing transformed into a commodity, and then into a vehicle for speculation, and when prices outran wages, people appeared on sidewalks and in doorways and in empty lots because the market that was supposed to house them had moved on to more profitable concerns. Walking through New Orleans Mid-City, I came across bright red graffiti on an abandoned house that read: Housing and homelessness equals society fails (Marina 2017). Someone wrote the analysis directly onto the wreckage it described.

The man sleeping in that doorway arrived there through those structural forces. Rents rise faster than wages. Affordable housing programs lose funding. Mental health facilities close without anything replacing them in the communities they leave behind. Most people stand closer to those circumstances than they admit, and they tend to identify with the politicians presiding over the conditions rather than with the neighbors dealing with them. Homelessness is a predictable outcome of society operating exactly as designed, and the man in the doorway deserves none of the blame for the structures that displaced him.

The law treats visibility as a problem to be managed in public areas. Officers enforce spatial boundaries, move people along, and protect property values while the conditions that produce sleeping outside remain unchanged. On reports and in conversation, words like transient and vagrant turn living people into categories of disorder rather than people in need of shelter. Stanley Cohen identified this as the construction of the folk devil, the figure a society loads with its anxieties and moves against as a substitute for addressing the conditions producing them (Cohen 1972/2011). George Orwell understood the same dynamic while living down and out in 1933 Paris and London, observing that it is fatal to look hungry, it makes people want to kick you (Orwell 2021). The man in the doorway sleeps in the only space available to him while rents rise, programs disappear, and the city continues forward without fixing the structural problems that cause homelessness.

The Question That Changes Everything

A human rights response begins with questions that separate immediate danger from economic discomfort. Has this person threatened anyone? Do they block access to the building? The business opens in two hours, which means obstruction is not a factor in the present situation. Did the caller speak to them directly? Is this private property or a public sidewalk?

That last question sets the legal foundation for everything that follows. A person resting on a public sidewalk exercises a lawful right. The dispatcher redirects the call toward that legal reality, explains to the caller that the concern they describe reflects discomfort, not a law violation, and points toward outreach services equipped to offer the man something more useful than a nudge toward the next block.

Which rights are implicated in this call? The right to life and security of person. The right to dignity. The right to equal protection. Those rights are embedded in how the dispatcher interprets what is being reported.

The Dispatch

Officers go out on a welfare check. A man rests in a doorway on a public sidewalk outside a business that opens in two hours. The situation presents no threats or crimes. Outreach services are on the way. That framing offers officers a person to help and establishes that the man on the sidewalk remains there until an actual violation occurs.

What gets recorded extends the response into the institutional file. The entry notes a welfare check, records the offer of outreach services, and states the basis for leaving the man in place. Months later, a supervisor reviewing the call sees a documented pattern of requests for removal without legal grounds, or a record that shows consistency in how the department distinguishes between poverty and law violation.

The Right to Exist

Repeated displacement drains department resources and leaves the man in the doorway where he started, only more exhausted, more exposed, and less certain that any area in this city is available to him even temporarily. Moving someone from one doorway to the next resolves nothing and produces a cost that falls on the person being moved.

The man sleeping in that doorway arrives this morning with full rights to public existence. Those rights do not depend on permission from the business owner who finds his presence uncomfortable, and they do not disappear because the system has grown used to treating visible poverty as disorder. He sleeps in a doorway on a public street. The dispatcher decides whether the response is a welfare check with outreach support, or another relocation that leads directly back into the same condition.

Scenario VII: When the Officer Asks for Something Wrong

Mr. Raymond

A family member sent me this story about his experience jogging in his residential neighborhood in St. Louis. This story sets the scene establishing the basis for this last scenario.

The situation that arises asks the dispatcher to push back against someone with formal authority over them. It's professionally risky to question a civilian, especially when a call is mishandled. It's even riskier to question an officer, regardless of the outcome.

The Fourth Amendment protections at stake in a stop depend on how the dispatcher frames the response. Facilitating a stop without reasonable suspicion participates in a civil rights violation, exposes the department to liability, and adds more weight to an already extensive record civil rights abuses. The dispatcher decides whether to interrupt that pattern or allow it to continue.

The Story

Mr. Raymond goes out for a St. Louis jog late one summer night. His story follows:

> I was out for a jog. Nighttime was conducive for jogging because it was cool and I liked the solitude. Turning onto Manchester Road, I see about 100 feet ahead a car parked, blocking my path. As I approached, I saw it was a used BMW. Having no choice but to go around it, I stared and noticed a 'for sale' sign in the passenger window. Having once driven a BMW but with no intent to ever own one, I approached slowly and checked it out. Hmm, I thought. OK. I walked away. Within seconds lights flashed, PO-PO. They were efficient and annoying. The sight of a middle-aged colored man peeking inside of a car for sale truly frightened them. I guess they thought I had my boost tools inside my jogging shorts and planned to make a fast getaway.
>
> The officer approached me from behind right after he turned on lights on his squad car. I was surprised. He boldly walked up and asked if I was casing the car. I responded that there was a for sale sign in the window. He then asked me to put my hands out and asked if I had any needles on me. I said I was much too old for that. About that time his partner, in another car, came up. He frisked me and then they both left.

He answered an accusation with wit and walked away with his dignity intact, which is more than the encounter deserved.

While Mr. Raymond stood on that sidewalk with his hands out, a patrol officer had already reached for the radio. The radio opens and the officer requests a warrant check. The request carries a familiar subtext: Does Not Belong Here. Those four words contain no description of criminal activity, observed violation, or articulable fact that meets any legal standard. They hold judgment disguised as concern, a pretext for suspicion resting on the assertion that a Black man's presence in a predominantly white neighborhood constitutes grounds for intervention. The dispatcher hears more than a request. They hear an attempt to turn presence into cause, and they decide what happens next.

Name. Warrant Check. Done.

The radio hums while the dispatcher types the name, runs the check, and relays the result. The stop moved forward without friction, mechanical and quiet, as if nothing consequential had just happened. The jogger experienced something different. He stood with his hands out while someone decided what kind of man he was. Each glance he casts now lands under a different standard, a judgment, the awareness that someone decided his presence required explanation. Of course, jogging while black, like walking or driving while black, has never met the legal threshold for reasonable suspicion, yet it is sometimes treated as if it does. Dispatchers who relay such requests without question make that framing operational. The dispatcher connects the officer's request with the man on the sidewalk, and what is transmitted through that process determines both the police response and how the encounter is defined when it begins.

The History the Radio Holds

The subtext of the officer's request – Does Not Belong Here – arrives at the dispatcher's station loaded with centuries of Black experiences with America's power structures. Slave patrols stopped Black people moving without authorization. Vagrancy laws criminalized Black mobility after emancipation. Stop-and-frisk policies subjected Black and brown people to mass detention while white residents moved through the same streets unfettered. That history arrives embedded in the assumption that a Black man jogging through a neighborhood where he is unexpected, stopping to look at a car with a for-sale sign, owes someone an explanation for being there. A dispatcher who hears that subtext and runs the check without question extends that history one more transaction at a time.

Officers have an authority that makes pushback professionally risky. But the dispatcher retains the responsibility to protect human rights and asks what is at stake here and what does the situation require.

The answers are precise.

The dispatcher asks the officer to describe what they observed. When the officer says the person was jogging and stopped to look at a car for sale, that answer becomes the record. It documents that no violation occurred, that no reasonable suspicion existed, and that the request proceeded without legal foundation. In agencies where direct questioning brings consequences, the same work moves through documentation. The dispatcher records what the person did, which was to jog and look at a car with a for-sale sign, and what the officer provided as justification, which was a judgment about belonging. Accuracy over time accomplishes something that goes beyond what a single exchange achieves alone. It renders the pattern visible to anyone who later examines what the record says.

A dispatcher who slows the process and asks what the officer observed protects both the jogger and the officer, because a stop conducted without reasonable suspicion exposes the officer to legal and disciplinary consequences that the moment of request often obscures. The officer may not recognize the risk embedded in what they ask the dispatcher. Asking for specific observed behavior before running the check functions as both a constraint on unlawful escalation and a safeguard for the officer's own exposure. Human rights dispatching holds requests to their legal threshold regardless of who makes them, and some requests fall outside that threshold even when issued in good faith.

Where the Decision Lives

This scenario asks more of the dispatcher than the others because the cost of getting it right sometimes falls on the dispatcher. The man jogging that night will never know what happened at the dispatch station in the seconds before the officer moved on. The dispatcher who asks the question, documents the exchange, and declines to facilitate a stop without legal foundation preserves a legal threshold the person it protects will never see.

Picture that man jogging down the block, unaware that a radio transmission went out with his name attached to it, unaware that someone a few miles away paused, asked a question, and wrote what was said into the record. He jogs to wherever he is going. The officer moves on. The dispatcher documents the encounter, capturing what was said and the standard it failed to meet. That record remains in the file, where it can be reviewed later, and where repeated entries begin to show what single calls do not reveal on their own.

The man on that sidewalk finishes his run. The dispatcher returns to the next call. Between those two moments, in the seconds when the radio crackled and the decision formed and the dispatcher chose what to record and how to frame it, a legal threshold was preserved that would otherwise have been lost.

Action Over Thoughts

A dispatcher hears a Somali accent and stops listening before the caller reaches the point. A dispatcher sees an address associated with frequent calls and assigns a lower priority before the caller describes what is happening. A dispatcher reads a name on the screen and expects a certain kind of problem before a word crosses the line. None of that deliberation happens in public. It happens in the two seconds between the ring and the answer, when the screen loads and the dispatcher constructs a version of the call the caller never gave.

This book does not tell you what to think, feel, or believe about race, immigration, mental illness, poverty, or anything else. Whatever sits in your mind belongs to you. This book does not attempt to correct it. What it addresses is what you do when the line opens and another person's safety, and human rights, depends on your next decision.

Human rights dispatching is action at the console. The tone that opens the exchange tells the caller in the first seconds how seriously their fear registers. The questions that follow determine how much of what happened survives the intake. The priority code determines how fast help moves. The framing sent to officers determines how they approach the door. The documentation becomes the official record of a person's worst moment, following them through every later encounter with the system. Each of these decisions affects someone who called because every other option failed.

This book does not require agreement, alignment, or the appearance of either. When a call comes through, whatever you believe stays with you. What happens on the line belongs to the person on the other end of it. Their safety depends on how you use your authority at the dispatch center. That authority operates under a human rights standard, regardless of what you think while you exercise it.

A woman sits in a parked car outside her apartment at two in the morning, both hands around her phone, the engine off, the street quiet, listening to the line ring. Something tonight drove her out of her home and into that car. She calls 911 because every other option failed. What she hears when you answer tells her what calling cost and what it returned. Your voice is the only help she has, at least until she sees headlights turn onto her street.

Whatever assumptions, reactions, and private judgments you brought into the shift stay there. What you say on the call shapes someone else's life after your shift ends. If the name, the accent, or the neighborhood were different, would the response remain the same? The person on the other end of the line already knows. Keep whatever thoughts you wish. Actions that protect human rights matter most.

The Person at the Dispatch Center

Seven scenarios, seven calls, and the same thing at stake each time. A person on the other end of the line reaching for a voice they can trust. Fear, confusion, pain, and urgency pass through that same channel.

Scripts do not get you through what Donna Choufani navigated in those five minutes. Checklists do not tell you to ask a 5-year-old about her black lab while deputies head to her front door. What gets you there is something you build in each call until it stops feeling like a discipline and starts feeling like the only way to work the line. What rights does this person bring into this moment? What does this situation require? What would I want if I were the one who had run out of options and reached for the phone in the dark?

That last question travels furthest. Donna Choufani asked it without asking it, working a five-minute call with a 5-year-old girl who had walked into her parents' bedroom and found blood on the floor. Choufani never reduced Tia Hernlen to a caller with a problem. She kept a child anchored in the world, talking about a black lab named Lizzah and a pink door her mother had picked out, until the deputy's headlights turned onto the street. This goes beyond technique. It shows what it looks like when a dispatcher understands, at a level beneath procedure, that the person on the other end deserves to be seen fully and protected completely, whatever the call costs and however long it takes.

Queues will stretch and shifts will run long. Easier paths will keep presenting themselves, call after call, across every shift. The question is whether you will keep asking what the person on the other end needs and deserves, and whether your answer will hold steady when the pressure to move on pushes hardest against it.

References

Bourgois, Philippe. 2003. *In Search of Respect: Selling Crack in El Barrio*. 2nd ed. Cambridge: Cambridge University Press.

Cohen, Stanley. 2011. *Folk Devils and Moral Panics: The Creation of the Mods and Rockers*. Routledge Classics ed. Abingdon: Routledge. Originally published 1972.

Du Bois, W. E. B. 1903. *The Souls of Black Folk*. Chicago: A. C. McClurg & Co.

Marina, Peter. 2017. *Down and Out in New Orleans: Transgressive Living in the Informal Economy*. New York: Columbia University Press.

Orwell, George. *Down and Out in Paris and London*. S.l.: Arcturus Publishing LTD, 2021.

Rogers, Michael S., Dale E. McNiel, and Renée L. Binder. 2019. "Effectiveness of Police Crisis Intervention Training Programs." *Journal of the American Academy of Psychiatry and the Law* 47 (4). https://doi.org/10.29158/JAAPL.003863-19.

Volusia County Sheriff's Office. 2005. "911 Call Transcript: Tia Hernlen." Released publicly by the Volusia County Sheriff. Archived April 17, 2015. https://web.archive.org/web/20150417192308/http://www.911dispatch.com/info/hernlen_choufani_transcript.html.

Chapter 6

The Long Game

Institutions, Dispatchers, and the Work That Remains

The dispatcher returns to the same room. The console still flashes with incoming calls. Supervisors and quality assurance staff review handle time through reports and call audits. The system still evaluates performance through clearance rates and protocol adherence. Nothing at work rewards staying on the line, challenging a biased call, or hearing what the caller speaks around.

The events across this book – the Philadelphia sidewalk, the Bergen Street sword, Donna Choufani and Tia Hernlen, the mother outside the locked bathroom door – circle the same question. How long can you keep making ethical decisions inside a system built to push you toward speed, compliance, and silence?

Human rights dispatching is a direction, not a destination. It requires conscious judgment on the days when the queue runs long, the shift has already gone hard, and every easier path points somewhere else.

The Institutional Problem

Every scenario in Chapter 5 revealed dispatcher agency, the power to choose differently, to frame a situation with thoughtfulness and accuracy. The frequent caller required a dispatcher who could hear the 16th call as clearly as the first, despite organizational pressure toward efficiency and rapid call resolution. The language barrier required a dispatcher who would remain engaged through repetition and frustration when ending the call quickly would have been easier to document. The walking while Black scenario required a dispatcher who could recognize how bias can shape interpretation of behavior and still risk being questioned in a review for deviating from expected neutrality or tone. The locked bathroom required a dispatcher who would slow the interaction, extract meaning from limited information, and resist the pull of performance metrics that later evaluate efficiency through recorded timestamps and audit review.

DOI: 10.4324/9781003583868-6

Communication centers, like most public safety institutions, organize themselves around response time, liability reduction, and procedural consistency. Supervisors and quality assurance staff review recorded calls and assess compliance with required questioning, documentation standards, and system codes. Performance reviews incorporate metrics such as call answer time, handling time distributions, and clearance measures tied to dispatch outcomes.

The caller experiences the difference between a dispatcher who recognizes their humanity and one who reduces the interaction to completion. The dispatcher who exercises that care inside an institution that ignores it will face structural pressure over time. Sustained human rights dispatching requires institutions to decide what they value and align training, evaluation, and promotion with that decision.

What Communication Centers Must Become

Human rights dispatching demands more than a training module squeezed between radio procedures and CAD updates, a certification box checked once a year, or a poster fading on a break room wall. Human rights centered communication centers build training around ethics. New dispatchers learn the sociological imagination and verstehen as operational tools before their first call arrives. Scenario work examines bias, language, and decision pressure. Quality assurance reviews for call framing and communication choices alongside protocol adherence. Supervision asks what the caller needed and how the interaction served them.

Current evaluations generally ask whether dispatchers collect the required information, code calls correctly, dispatch within target time, and follow protocol (Association of Public-Safety Communications Officials [APCO] and National Emergency Number Association [NENA] 2015). Human rights centered evaluations ask those questions and add others. Did the dispatcher preserve the caller's dignity during the interaction? Did they allow the caller to speak without unnecessary interruption? Did they send information to responding units in language that avoided loaded or speculative framing? Did they recognize and mitigate bias in caller reports when it appeared? Did they exercise appropriate discretion when rigid protocol did not fully match the situation unfolding in real time?

Consider a mental health crisis call where the dispatcher codes correctly, dispatches within target time, and follows every protocol. Under current standards, the call passes. Under a human rights centered standard, it fails if the dispatcher frames the situation as a potentially violent subject without behavioral indicators and transmits that framing to responding units before gathering sufficient context. Such language decides how responders perceive the situation before they arrive, narrowing the range of possible approaches.

Leadership determines whether this framework survives contact with daily pressure. A supervisor who removes a dispatcher from the floor because a call extended beyond expected handling time, or who treats sustained engagement with a suicidal teenager as inefficiency, signals the institution's actual priorities with unmistakable clarity. Declarations about dignity collapse when supervisors discipline the time required to uphold it.

Communities that experience the downstream effects of dispatch decisions, including inconsistent framing, uneven response pathways, and breakdowns in communication, deserve formal avenues to raise concerns, review patterns, and demand accountability. Public institutions exist to serve the people and their community. Their participation sustains the legitimacy that makes emergency calling possible at all.

Mobile crisis teams and co-responder models now respond alongside or in place of officers in many jurisdictions. In Denver and San Francisco, access to these models depends heavily on dispatch decision-making at the point of call intake (Gillooly and Friedman 2026). The communication center sits at the hinge of these systems.

The dispatcher who routes a mental health call to a crisis team when criteria and availability allow, who treats substance-use calls as health emergencies, who connects a person experiencing homelessness to outreach resources, exercises human rights dispatching in its most consequential form. That capacity requires training, protocols, and system resources the institution must provide. Institutions that treat it as individual improvisation make a structural decision about which crises receive care and which receive force.

The Technology Arriving at the Dispatch Center

Every call a dispatcher handles moves through the Computer-Aided Dispatch system, the software that receives calls, logs information, recommends units, tracks response times, and creates a permanent record of each interaction. CAD forms the technological architecture through which dispatcher judgment travels.

Michel Foucault understood the panopticon not as a building but as a principle (Foucault 1975/1977). Jeremy Bentham designed a circular prison in which a single guard could observe every inmate without the inmates knowing when observation occurred (Bentham 1787–1791/2011). Foucault focused on the logic, not the structure. When people believe observation may occur at any moment, they begin to regulate themselves. Surveillance becomes internal. Compliance arises from the constant possibility of scrutiny. Foucault argued in Discipline and Punish that this principle migrated from the prison into schools, hospitals, factories, and military institutions. Power did not depend on continuous watching. The possibility shaped conduct (Foucault 1975/1977).

The architecture of surveillance has since expanded far beyond what Foucault analyzed. In 2013, Edward Snowden revealed that the National Security Agency had constructed a system of large-scale data collection that gathered phone metadata and digital communications from millions of individuals who were not suspected of criminal activity (Greenwald 2013; Privacy and Civil Liberties Oversight Board 2014). Snowden disclosed these programs and subsequently fled the United States, exposing the extent to which mass surveillance had become embedded within contemporary governance (Greenwald 2014). The disclosure described the infrastructure of a democratic government turned toward its own people.

The dispatcher sits inside that ecosystem. Tools originally designed for counterterrorism, battlefield intelligence, and national security operations have migrated steadily into domestic law enforcement and, from there, into emergency communication. Data aggregation platforms built to track foreign adversaries now cross-reference the records of American residents. Companies that manufacture body cameras and conducted energy weapons have acquired emergency communications technology, embedding real-time geolocation, live video capture, and behavioral analytics into the infrastructure of the 911 call. The branding around these acquisitions emphasizes faster response and saved lives. The architecture they install reaches into the most vulnerable moment of a person's life, the moment they pick up the phone to ask for help, and it does so without their meaningful knowledge or consent. The pace of that expansion shows no sign of slowing, and the regulatory frameworks governing what that data becomes, where it travels, and who can access it have not kept pace with the technology producing it.

Governments have long been able to purchase location data, browsing history, and political affiliations on private citizens from commercial data brokers. That practice has always been technically legal. The data existed in scattered, disconnected silos that required enormous human labor to assemble into a coherent picture of any individual life. Artificial intelligence removes that barrier. It makes it possible to aggregate what were once scattered and individually innocuous data points into a comprehensive portrait of any person, automatically, continuously, and at an unprecedented scale across populations (Zuboff 2019). The law has not kept pace with what the technology now makes possible, and when legal permission falls behind technical capacity, rights erode in practice without any explicit decision to remove them.

Surveillance embedded in the call reaches the person before the dispatcher does, and that person already calculates whether calling is safe. The caller experiencing double consciousness, the immigrant fearing deportation, the person in mental health crisis fearing forced hospitalization, and the sex worker expecting punishment without protection all weigh that risk before dialing. When the call connects and the data collection begins, it confirms what they already fear: that the system will use what they share against them. The panopticon at the level of emergency communication produces silence that keeps people in crisis from calling.

Predictive policing tools trained on historical enforcement data can't forecast crime. They reproduce patterns of prior deployment. Research has documented that these algorithms use variables like zip code, socioeconomic background, and prior arrest history as proxies for race, producing outputs that are functionally racially biased regardless of their stated neutrality (Richardson, Schultz, and Crawford 2019; O'Donnell 2019). When those predictions feed into call prioritization or unit recommendation, dispatcher agency contracts. The algorithm suggests. The dispatcher confirms. The decision is already made. The logic hides inside proprietary software that the public cannot examine and the community never chose.

The distinction worth drawing separates tools that expand human judgment from systems designed for surveillance and rebranded as service. Beyond operational decision-making, dispatch is embedded in broader systems of data extraction and surveillance that shape how calls are processed before human judgment is fully exercised. What arrived as counterterrorism infrastructure and departed as public safety technology brought its original logic with it, and the people calling for help never consented to living inside it.

Artificial intelligence will continue entering emergency communication. Does the system enhance human judgment, or does it replace and surveil it? A tool that informs and leaves the decision in human hands supports agency. A system that dictates outcomes through opaque algorithms, captures sensitive personal data during a crisis call, and routes that data through networks the dispatcher never sees shifts authority away from the dispatcher, away from the caller, and away from the community the center exists to serve.

It's important for communication center leaders and frontline dispatchers to press vendors and administrators on what every new system is designed to do, whose data it uses, and how that data moves beyond the dispatch environment, whether it shapes call classification before a human reviews anything, and whether the community served by the center has any visibility into how it operates. This reflects the increasing complexity of dispatch systems and the constraints they place on decision-making (Gillooly and Friedman 2026). Unanswered questions about design, data, and accountability are governance failures, and institutions that accept them have made a choice about whose interests the system serves.

Thirty Years on the Job

My father spent 30 years in law enforcement. His career began with him holding the head of a dying man on his third day in uniform. Accumulation defines the profession. The calls that remain long after the shift ends. The calls where the right decision still ends badly. The calls where attention was incomplete. The cost to the person, on the other end, remains. The shifts that erode something slowly enough that erosion feels like hardening. Professional detachment slides into indifference, so gradually the shift rarely announces itself.

Georg Simmel described the blasé attitude as a psychological adaptation to relentless stimuli and suffering (Simmel 1903/2002). As described in Chapter 2, my father, Pedro Marina, spent 30 years with the New Orleans Police Department tracing this transformation across hundreds of calls, beginning on his third day in uniform and accumulating until detachment became the only available form of survival. Dispatchers develop a quieter version of the same pattern. They remain in one place and absorb crisis through a headset, hour after hour, year after year, without the physical interruption that sometimes allows field officers brief release or reset. The stillness conceals the strain. No incident report marks the moment it begins.

Communication centers should treat psychological injury as an occupational reality and design response systems accordingly. Debriefing and counseling need to be part of the baseline professional standard, available to every dispatcher as routine support rather than ad hoc intervention. Supervisors should conduct structured check-ins that invite candid responses and create conditions where honesty does not carry professional risk. Agencies also need to fund and formalize peer support programs so they extend beyond informal, voluntary conversations and become an integrated part of workplace infrastructure.

No one can protect the rights of others from a place of depletion. When institutions extract decades of emotional labor without structured support or processing, they weaken the judgment they depend on. A dispatcher who brings 20 years of unresolved exposure, who has worked without time for reflection, and who has learned that survival requires emotional withdrawal will struggle to sustain human rights-centered dispatching.

The Work That Remains

Debates over defunding, reform, abolition, community control, and the role of law enforcement in a democratic society continue. Whatever shape policing takes, the dispatcher remains the hinge between a person in crisis and the system's response.

The calls continue. A frequent caller returns. A mother speaks through a locked door. A woman lowers her voice while danger waits in the next room. A teenager describes pain that resists relief. A man reports a presence outside his home. A person without shelter sleeps in a doorway and someone requests removal. An officer requests action that places rights at stake. Each cycle returns to the dispatcher where one person determines what follows.

Human rights dispatching begins before any officer steps out of a vehicle. It begins in language that defines a situation, in tone that steadies panic, in questions that restore a person from category to presence, and in dispatch decisions that direct response toward assistance. It begins with a dispatcher who recognizes that authority at the dispatch center extends into outcomes, and that every call presents a chance to use it with care.

This book speaks to dispatchers who stay on the line beyond the limits of a metric, who interrupt bias before it moves through the radio, who hear fear and respond with steadiness and patience. It speaks to the dispatcher who treats the 16th call with the same attention as the first because earlier calls never resolved what brought the caller back.

The dispatcher sees a person before a call, hears fear beneath language, and answers with steadiness, attention, and skill. Beneath procedure, the dispatcher understands that human rights move with every call and remain present until the line goes quiet. It lives in the dispatcher who listens to a trembling voice long enough for meaning to form, who reads a screen without letting a label replace a person, and who determines what language moves forward into the field.

At two in the morning, the dispatch center hums under dim light as three calls wait in the queue. On one line, a woman speaks so quietly the room around her seems to hold its breath. On another, a teenager searches for words to describe a relentless pain that refuses to subside. On a third, a man reports someone lingering outside his home. Three people who called because there was nowhere else to turn, and one dispatcher at the console who decides what happens next.

At the end, as at the start, the human rights dispatcher decides.

References

Association of Public-Safety Communications Officials (APCO) and National Emergency Number Association (NENA). 2015. *Standard for the Establishment of a Quality Assurance and Quality Improvement Program for Public Safety Answering Points (APCO/NENA ANS 1.107.1–2015)*. Daytona Beach, FL: APCO International.

Bentham, Jeremy. 2011. *The Panopticon Writings*. edited by Miran Božovič. 2nd ed. London: Verso. Originally published 1787–1791.

Foucault, Michel. 1977. *Discipline and Punish: The Birth of the Prison*. Translated by Alan Sheridan. New York: Pantheon Books. Originally published 1975.

Gillooly, Jessica W., and Barry Friedman. 2026. "Rethinking Rules for 911: Dispatching Alternative Responders in Denver and San Francisco." *Criminology & Public Policy*. https://doi.org/10.1111/1745-9133.70008.

Greenwald, Glenn. 2013. "NSA Collecting Phone Records of Millions of Verizon Customers Daily." *The Guardian*, June 6, 2013. https://www.theguardian.com/world/2013/jun/06/nsa-phone-records-verizon-court-order.

Greenwald, Glenn. 2014. *No Place to Hide: Edward Snowden, the NSA, and the U.S. Surveillance State*. New York: Metropolitan Books.

O'Donnell, Christopher. 2019. "Challenging Racist Predictive Policing Algorithms under the Equal Protection Clause." *NYU Law Review* 94 (3): 544–85.

Privacy and Civil Liberties Oversight Board. 2014. *Report on the Telephone Records Program Conducted under Section 215 of the USA PATRIOT Act and on the Operations of the Foreign Intelligence Surveillance Court*. Washington, DC. https://www.pclob.gov/library/215-Report_on_the_Telephone_Records_Program.pdf.

Richardson, Rashida, Jason M. Schultz, and Kate Crawford. 2019. "Dirty Data, Bad Predictions: How Civil Rights Violations Impact Police Data, Predictive Policing Systems, and Justice." *NYU Law Review Online* 94. https://www.nyulawreview.org/online-features/dirty-data-bad-predictions/.

Simmel, Georg. 2002. "The Metropolis and Mental Life." In *The Blackwell City Reader*, edited by Gary Bridge and Sophie Watson, 11–19. Oxford: Wiley-Blackwell. Originally published 1903.

Zuboff, Shoshana. 2019. *The Age of Surveillance Capitalism: The Fight for a Human Future at the New Frontier of Power*. New York: PublicAffairs.

Index

For Product Safety Concerns and Information please contact our EU representative GPSR@taylorandfrancis.com Taylor & Francis Verlag GmbH, Kaufingerstraße 24, 80331 München, Germany